Thinking Historically

Dutchess County Historical Society
Centennial Celebration
1914 – 2014

Dutchess County Historical Society
2014 Yearbook • Volume 93

Candace J. Lewis, *Editor*

Dutchess County Historical Society

Publications Committee:

Candace J. Lewis, Ph.D., *Editor*
Roger Donway, Deborah Golomb, Eileen Hayden
Julia Hotton, Melodye Moore

Designer: Marla Neville, Main Printing
www.mymainprinter.com

Printer: NetPub, Inc. www.netpub.net

Dutchess County Historical Society Yearbook 2014
Volume 93 • Published annually since 1915
Copyright © by Dutchess County Historical Society
ISSN: 0739-8565
ISBN: 978-0-944733-09-7

Cover: An outing to the Residence of Isaac S. Wheaton, Lithgow, NY,
by the Dutchess County Historical Society September 15, 1926.
Detail: Photograph (panoramic). Collection of the
Dutchess County Historical Society.

The Society is a not-for-profit educational organization that collects,
preserves, and interprets the history of Dutchess County, New York,
from the period of the arrival of the first Native Americans
until the present day.

Dutchess County Historical Society

Dutchess County Historical Society
P.O. Box 88
Poughkeepsie, NY 12602
845-471-1630
Email: dchistorical@verizon.net

www.dutchesscountyhistoricalsociety.org

This issue of the Dutchesss County Historical Society's
yearbook has been generously underwritten by the following:

Congratulations to the
Dutchess County Historical Society
and Happy Birthday: 100 years old.

Anonymous

Congratulations to the
Dutchess County Historical Society
for its one hundred years of effort
to preserve and communicate our region's past.

Roger and Alisan Donway

Shirley M. Handel

LTC Gilbert A. Krom

One hundred years and still going strong.
Hooray!

·

Lou and Candace J. Lewis

❧

Leonard E. and Sandra S. Opdycke

Kimberley Jones, View of the Hudson River from the Mid-Hudson Bridge, looking south. May 2014. Acrylic on canvas.

Table of Contents

ADDENDA

Foreword

by Marcus J. Molinaro,
County Executive, Dutchess County

As Dutchess County enters her 301st year of democracy, we look back on three centuries of local achievements. Among the significant anniversaries this year is the Dutchess County Historical Society's centennial, a landmark event that reminds us of our deep historical roots and the bright future we are building upon them. The society's achievements over the past hundred years mirror those of the county as a whole, as does the society's promise for future excellence. Through its on-going programs and many contributions, the Dutchess County Historical Society has worked to define who we are as a people and how we hope to live.

Since its inception, the Dutchess County Historical Society has been an inspirational model for preserving and promoting our community heritage. Through the collection of irreplaceable documents and artifacts that showcase daily life in the county and sharing the stories these items tell through exhibits, tours, and other programming, the society has kept memories of old Dutchess alive. We continue to follow this example today with projects such as our Dutchess County Government Exhibit on the 6th Floor of the County Office Building at 22 Market Street in Poughkeepsie.

One of the society's most outstanding achievements over the past hundred years has been the continuous publication of the Dutchess County Historical Society Yearbook. Few history organizations nationwide can compete with that record, adding to the list of unique and innovative achievements that have long issued forth from Dutchess County. The Yearbook and the society's look back over its first hundred years further reminds us that we are making history today. What we achieve in the present and the marks we leave on our community now are tomorrow's history and lay the groundwork and example for future excellence.

Just as the society now considers the lessons of its first hundred years and looks to the future, so do we as a county community re-invest in our past achievements and set the stage for future excellence. Our recent renovation of Dutchess Stadium continues a twenty year commitment to providing affordable family entertainment to our community. Our continuing transformation of county government is creating a model of new efficiency through workforce enhancement and the creation of unique new solutions to today's challenges. As we move forward together as a county community, we insure that the Dutchess County Historical Society will have plenty of history to document and celebrate at its bicentennial.

After all, it is who we are and how we hope to live.

Introduction

by William P. Tatum III,
Dutchess County Historian

The Dutchess County Historical Society's centennial reminds us of New York Public History's origins in the opening decades of the twentieth century. The nation's centennial in 1876 combined with the need to heal over the schisms of civil war introduced a new phase of patriotic historical fervor in the closing decades of the nineteenth century. For Dutchess County in particular, that interest took form as the Dutchess County Society in the City of New York, about which you may read further thanks to an article by Melodye Moore in this edition. While we cannot yet draw a causal link between that organization and the Dutchess County Historical Society of today, the former's existence testifies to the long-standing interest in our county's heritage.

The Gilded Age celebrations had increased awareness of the fragility of the historical record at the same time as they celebrated it, generating a new push for the collection and preservation of documents and artifacts. Thus the county historical society's creation was as much a reaction to the needs of documentation and preservation as it was to the general celebratory spirit of the age. Founded a few short years before the Historian's Law of 1919, which created our system of government historians, the Dutchess County Historical Society and its counterparts statewide have provided the foundation for a public-private partnership that has increasingly shaped our approach to history. In many respects, the history of the society has been the history of our county community, for without this institution, we would have few records and little understanding of daily life in the county.

As we look back to 1914, we see the unmistakable stamp left by generations of society members in preserving and promoting the county's personal history. Through its collecting activities, the society has insured the survival of resources from the 1702 lintel stone of the Van Kleek House, among Poughkeepsie's earliest dwellings, to a unique document collection chronicling 150 years of Dutchess County apple growing. The society's public programming, ranging from the annual gala to the Road Rallye, has increased access to the county's historical sites and celebrated our historians' achievements. The Yearbook's outstanding record of 100 years of unbroken publication offers an unparalleled reservoir of local history knowledge and an example of editorial excellence to be admired. With such a strong foundation to build upon, we can all look forward to another century of success for Dutchess County History with our historical society in the lead.

Letter from the Editor

One hundred years before the time of this writing in August 2014, the Dutchess County Historical Society was a fledgling organization. On April 28, 1914, fifty motivated people from various locations in Dutchess County had gathered in the Pleasant Valley Free Library to form the society. That August has been described as

> the most terrible August in the history of the world. One might have thought already that God's curse hung heavy over a degenerate world, for there was an awesome hush and a feeling of vague expectancy in the sultry and stagnant air. [1]

Certainly, our new local members were cognizant of the fact that, at that point, fifty years after the Civil War, they had to take action if they were to have any hope of preserving letters, diaries, and other documents associated with that most important event in American history. Were they aware of the war looming in their future? By August, when the air was mild, but reports of the assassination of Archduke Franz Ferdinand of Austria-Hungary were generating heated editorials in the newspapers, did they anticipate the next four-and-a-half years of destruction? Perhaps not, but certainly, in this suspended moment, they had chosen the right path by dedicating themselves to preserving the history of Dutchess County.

To mark the centenary of the Dutchess County Historical Society, we have selected the theme, "Thinking Historically," friendly words that we often use as part of a farewell at the end of meetings: "let's all keep thinking historically." It is said in a light-hearted way. But, what do we think of when we turn our minds to history? For many, the very word, "history,"conjures up a vision of fellows in funny looking trousers, high collars, or ladies in unusually shaped skirts speaking in extremely stilted speech. For some, history can mean lessons from the past to help us lead our lives today. There will be very little of either here. In the pages of this yearbook, we have tried to address the question of history sometimes directly, sometimes obliquely—but always looking for as clear a picture of the past as we can evoke.

The Forum section is devoted to the topic "Thinking Historically"—first in the thoughtful essay by Denise Van Buren where she writes about her interest in New York State and Dutchess County history, in articles by Leo Opdycke and Harvey Flad where they approach the topic through their bodies of knowledge about aviation and photography, and in a story told by David Johnson about the celebration of the Armistice of World War I in

1928 where narrative prevails. Finally, in the Forum section, we are proud to offer new research by Julia Hotton in her essay about African-Americans and the Union Army.

The Articles section presents three essays on a variety of topics: on a young man of northern Dutchess who was not able to fight in the Civil War, but left a legacy to his town (by Cynthia Koch); on world-renowned photographer, Lee Miller (by Lou Lewis); and on a photograph of the Poughkeepsie railroad station (by Mary-Kay Lombino).

The Centennial Celebration section is our offering specifically aimed at the 100th birthday of the society. It begins with a history of the Dutchess County Historical Society by Eileen Hayden, continues with a newly researched account of a parallel institution in New York City by Melodye Moore, is followed by a discussion of Franklin D. Roosevelt and his approach to history by Bob Clark, and concludes with a short biography of one of the early members of the society by Caroline Reichenberg. These essays are followed by a series of short accounts, chiefly by town historians or heads of local historical societies, relating the stories of families or businesses that have been in continuous operation in Dutchess County from 1914 to 2014, the same period that the Dutchess County Historical Society has been in existence. Let's all enjoy history. Let us all think historically.

— *Candace Jenks Lewis*

---

[1] Arthur Conan Doyle, "His Last Bow", in *The New Annotated Sherlock Holmes*, The Complete Short Stories, Vol. 2: *The Return of Sherlock Holmes, His Last Bow, and The Case-Book of Sherlock Holmes*, ed. Leslie S. Klinger (New York & London: W.H. Norton and Company, 2004), p.1424.

FORUM

Thinking Historically: My Take

by Denise Doring VanBuren

Why think historically? In an interconnected global society, why should regional history matter to anyone? Because it is our communal past that provides our sense of identity and then points each of us toward a destiny that is our own to shape. This past-to-present continuum is perhaps no-where more evident than here in New York State, where so many significant events have occurred and so much promise exists.

I grew up proudly knowing that generations of my family have lived along the Hudson for centuries. I believed that New York was the most exceptional state in the union. My parents acknowledged that we paid high taxes here, but they believed that we had, as a result, the best of everything—the very best highways, schools, cultural institutions—and the finest quality of life. We had a true sense of belonging to something larger, grander, and worthwhile.

Sadly, many New Yorkers seem no longer to feel that way about our state. How many of us are disappointed but not surprised to read that millions of people have left our state—all too often driven out, the media tell us, because of high taxes, a lack of jobs, or simply the lack of a compelling reason to stay here? As a parent, and a thirteenth-generation New Yorker, that saddens me.

New York State

Perhaps it is time to reconnect with our past, to remember what made our state, in the 1785 words of George Washington, "the seat of the Empire."[1] Perhaps if we all thought historically about our state, we would discover that its proud past holds the key to a very promising future indeed.

After all, New York State is home to Cooperstown, Saratoga, Niagara Falls, Lake Placid, and Chautauqua—unique and beautiful places whose very names conjure up magical historical and modern-day connections. New York City, with its 8.3 million people, is still the largest city in the nation (and the second largest, Los Angeles, has just 3.8 million residents). The Adirondack Park alone is the largest publicly protected area in the contiguous United States, greater in size than the Yellowstone, Everglades, Glacier, and Grand Canyon National Parks—combined!

And while the economy of our state struggles, it is far from moribund. New York's is a $1.16 trillion economy. Were we an independent nation, we would rank sixteenth in the world. New York still exports a wide variety of goods: food, commodities, minerals, computers and electronics, cut diamonds, and automobile parts. In fact, our state exports more $71 billion worth of goods annually.

Historically, of course, New York was always considered the strategic center of the colonial territories. Did you know that the British thought this colony so important that it was the only British territory in which troops were regularly stationed during the entire colonial period?

It was here in New York that Britain and France fought to gain control of our strategic location. It was in Albany that the first serious attempt to form an inter-colonial federation occurred: The Albany Plan of Union was proposed by Benjamin Franklin at the Albany Congress in 1754. It was an early attempt to form an alliance of the colonies "under one government as far as might be necessary for defense and other general important purposes" during the French and Indian War.[2]

During the American Revolution, nearly one third of all battles were fought here in New York. British strategy focused on the conquest of New York as the best way to split New England from the south and thus end the war quickly. A century earlier, British Governor Lord Bellomont wrote to his superiors, that New York "by its scituation [sic] (being much in the center of the other Colonies) challenges a preference to all the rest and ought to be looked upon as the capital Province or the Cittadel [sic] to all others; for secure but this, and you secure all the English Colonies, not only against the French, but also against any insurrections or rebellions against the Crown of England."[3] It is little wonder that New York was the key battleground of the American Revolution.

It was at Saratoga in 1777 that the most decisive battle between those of Lexington and Yorktown occurred. And it was from New York City that the British evacuated their remaining troops from the new United States when the war was over. New York then served as the capital of the United States from 1785 until 1790, and it was there that George Washington took his oath of office as our first president.

Our motto as the Empire State took on new meaning with the completion of the Erie Canal. Proposed in 1808 and completed in 1825, the canal linked the waters of Lake Erie in the west to the Hudson River in the east.

An engineering marvel when it was built, it was billed as the Eighth Wonder of the World. The canal fostered a population surge in western New York State, opened regions farther west to settlement, and helped New York City become the chief U.S. port. All of this benefitted our Hudson River communities, which lay along this path.

New Yorkers should be familiar with some of the other key events that changed the world's course and well illustrate our state's dramatic influence on American exceptionalism:

- 1792: The New York Stock Exchange is founded, making New York the center of world finance.

- 1802: The U.S. Military Academy opens at West Point.

- 1809: Robert Fulton's "North River Steamboat," the first successful steam-propelled vessel, begins a new era in transportation.

- 1812: Another war between the United States and Great Britain, fought largely in New York, ends in a stalemate but confirms America's Independence

- 1848: Elizabeth Cady Stanton, Lucretia Mott, and more than 300 women and men gather in Seneca Falls, for the nation's first women's rights convention.

- 1861–1865: During the Civil War, the State of New York supplies almost one-sixth of all Union forces, and many of the arms and goods that wins the war for the North.

- 1883: The Brooklyn Bridge, a wonder of design and engineering, opens.

- 1886: The Statue of Liberty (with its famous 1903 inscription, "Give me your tired, your poor, your huddled masses yearning to breathe free") becomes the first symbol of America seen by more than 12 million immigrants as they pass through Ellis Island until its closing in 1954.

- 1931: The Empire State Building and the Chrysler Building are completed, and the George Washington Bridge opened, all adding to New York City's astounding skyline.

- 1946: New York City is chosen as the site of the United Nations.

- 1959: The St. Lawrence Seaway opens.

By the 1960s, nearly fifteen percent of the entire nation's manufacturing jobs were located here in New York State. But things changed; times grew more difficult in the years to come as manufacturers, jobs, and people moved to the Sunbelt states. Between 1960 and 1980, 5,000 plant closings and contractions took place in New York State; half a million jobs were lost. During the decade of 1970 to 1980, New York's population declined by nearly 4 percent.

Yet the good news is that our population has been rebounding since that time. In fact, the 2010 census records show that New York State's population has grown by 2.1 percent since the year 2000. An estimated record of 19.6 million people now reside here in the Empire State. In January of 2014, Governor Cuomo reported: "[W]e've added 380,000 private sector jobs since 2010. New York is number two in jobs created since the recession [of 2008] ... We have more jobs today than at any time in history of the state of New York."

If we have, indeed, turned a corner, then why not now think historically to identify the resources and attributes that made us succeed in the past, in order to shape a prosperous future for this record number of inhabitants? To think historically so that New York State might once again be considered the seat of the empire?[1] Our people, climate, population, scenic beauty and strategic physical location all wait to be re-tapped by those who can envision a future built upon the strong foundation of the past.

Dutchess County, New York

The same approach can obviously be taken toward our own county of Dutchess. Historically, we have always benefitted from our proximity to New York City and all that its massive population attracts and demands. But within our own borders, we have also manufactured scores of products through the centuries—from hats to cough drops, from ovens to computers. We have planted violets and harvested apples; we have grown hops and delivered dairy products. We are the site of three successful universities and a vibrant community college, all of which built upon rich traditions to evolve into dynamic institutions of higher learning. We have world-class healthcare institutions and cultural institutions.

It was in Poughkeepsie, which served as our State's Capital in 1788, that New York State agreed to ratify the U.S. Constitution, providing the critical approval that ensured passage of our government's framework; it was also in Dutchess County that delegates hammered out compromise that both allowed for that approval and paved the way for our nation's Bill of Rights. New York Governor George Clinton, whose estate was located in the town of Poughkeepsie, was one of only two men who would serve two different presidents as their vice president. More than a century later, native son (and Dutchess County Historical Society founding member) Franklin D. Roosevelt would use his home as a summer White House and the location for the first Presidential Library. And, of course, only once has a single county produced both candidates in a presidential election, when FDR was challenged by Thomas E. Dewey, who lived in Pawling.

In truth, such interesting chapters and important sites of historic significance are all around us, waiting to inspire us. Dutchess County boasts 244 properties on the National Register of Historic Places. From Hyde Park to Hopewell, there are literally hundreds of historic structures and locations that the federal government has designated as national treasures, all of them here in Dutchess County.

In addition to our historical accomplishments, few places in the entire nation can boast of a more beautiful landscape. From the shores of the Hudson River and the peaks of the Hudson Highlands to the farmlands and forests of eastern and northern Dutchess, our scenic vistas are breathtaking in every season (Figure 1).

Figure 1. *A view of the schooner* Mystic Whaler, *sister ship to the sloop* Clearwater, *sailing before the Mid-Hudson Bridge on the Hudson River. A small, fast motorboat is carving a circle around the* Mystic Whaler. *Photo taken from a vantage point on the Walkway-over-the-Hudson by Fred Schaeffer, May 2014. Collection of Fred Schaeffer.*

Furthermore, we are rich in human resources. Ranked fifteenth in population in New York State counties, Dutchess has approximately 297,000 residents and has experienced the fifth highest rate of growth among counties in the state since the year 2000. We have the talented and committed people necessary to chart a course that will lead from our storied past to a vibrant future.

In 2014, we celebrate not only the centennial anniversary of the Dutchess County Historical Society but also the 350th anniversary of the 1664 transfer of New Netherlands from the Netherlands to England. The resulting formation of the "New York" colony, with Dutchess County as an integral part of its success, would be critical to the development of the new United States.

What will we contribute during the next 350 years? When we think historically, the possibilities appear limitless.

---

[1] In a 1785 letter, George Washington called New York "the Seat of the Empire." George Washington to New York City Officials and Citizens, April 10, 1785. George Washington Papers at the Library of Congress, 1741–1799: Series 3c Varick Transcripts. Letterbook 5, Images 182–84. http://memory.loc.gov/cgi-bin/ampage?collId=mgw3&-fileName=mgw3c/gwpage005.db&recNum=187&tempFile=./temp/~ammem_ODIl&-filecode=mgw&next_filecode=mgw&prev_filecode=mgw&itemnum=12&ndocs=100

[2] The plan represented one of multiple early attempts to form a union of the colonies "under one government as far as might be necessary for defense and other general important purposes." Benjamin Franklin, *The Autobiography of Benjamin Franklin, 2nd ed.* (New Haven, CT: Yale University Press, 1964), 209–10.

[3] E. B. O'Callaghan, *Documents relative to the Colonial History of the State of New-York, Vol. IV* (Albany, NY: Weed, Parsons and Company, 1854), p. 505

Watching Aviation in Dutchess County: Myth and Meaning, and Meaning and Myth

by Leonard E. Opdycke

The word "history" has come to have two senses, which in turn have come to overlap. The first meaning comprises the events, things, and changes that have occurred in the past; the second, what we have found out about them, through writings, records, fossils, DNA, and so forth. These findings, in turn, then become part of the history for the future. This paper will focus on early aviation in Dutchess County—but it will begin somewhere else.

Jane's All The World's Aircraft, 2013 published a statement by the Australian aero historian John Brown that Connecticut engineer Gustave Whitehead had flown in 1901, before the Wrights' famous flight in 1903. Naturally, there has been a lot of professional response to it.[1] One way of exploring this issue is to think of the two accounts—Whitehead's and the Wrights'—as myths. We generally think of the word "myth" as a description of a story or a view of the world that captures the imagination and affects the behavior of some people: we have often observed the power of myth when it affects other, often more "primitive" societies. But we rarely recognize how often our own lives are shaped by our own myths.

In fact, we might say that our whole sense of the world is a myth—developed accurately or inaccurately from the daily activities of our senses regarding the events in the world around us, including other people and the world itself. Our minds and bodies help us as much as they know how, and as much as we let them, but they are not always reliable. Even so, these interpretations represent all we know about the world—and about ourselves, since we really exist only in terms of how we experience our bodies and minds and the world around us.

Wherever a myth exists—whether among the ancient Greeks or among the residents of Wappingers Falls today, it has three characteristics: it explains something (rightly or wrongly!) in the world; it gives some sense of control and involvement with it; and it provides some basis for social or community activities with which to work and live. A myth is a social experience. It encourages interactions among us all: watching, observing, noticing more closely; asking questions where possible; wondering about, rather than knowing, the right answers.

Figure 1. *Leo Opdycke flying his Bristol Scout over Rhinebeck, New York: first flight, 1983. Leo built this aeroplane as a reproduction of the original 1914 Bristol Scout D with an original LeRhone rotary engine. Photograph by Bill Hammond. Collection of Leonard E. Opdycke.*

Flight has always been a compelling myth, affording people opportunities to watch, to imitate, to participate in, or to describe—and to dream. In this article I'll be exploring some of the ways this myth has attracted attention and activity in Dutchess County over the years leading to various forms of historical recording and preserving that luckily remain for us. This article represents only the latest one—and in itself not only discusses myth, but joins it and carries it forward.

History and "Myth"

The questions remain: "What actually did happen?" "What *is* the historical truth?" Most recent conversations about the Whitehead-Wright problem have been aimed at trying to answer the questions: "Who flew first?" and "What are the facts Involved?" Looking these over, I am reminded of my experience as a juror in a malpractice case here in Poughkeepsie back in 1994. The judge said before the trial began that we should remember that with all the reports and photos that the prosecution and the defense would show us as evidence, upon which we would have to base our final decision, there would not be a single fact among them. The only fact in the room would appear when we the jury arrived at a final story. We did finally arrive at a Fact—but in the case of that trial, not quite where some of us had hoped to arrive. Maybe in the case of many of these historical puzzles, the jury may never come back!

In literal terms, either the Wrights or Whitehead flew first. And yet each competing claim has a larger mythic quality. Think of the web of associations and drama we have constructed around the idea of the Wrights as

Figure 2. *Aerial view of the intersection at Red Oaks Mill, in the Town of Poughkeepsie, New York. Vassar Road (running from the lower left to the upper right in the image) crossed by Spackenkill Road (running from the upper left across the picture plane). Modern-day Route 376, the curvy road, runs down the right through the trees. The hangar of the airport (first called the Spackenkill Airport, later called the Poughkeepsie Airport) is visible at the side of Vassar Road, near the intersection. c. 1927–1930. Photograph by Jack Ray. Collection of Peter Colomello.*

First Flyers—the excitement of that morning at Kitty Hawk, the museum exhibitions that celebrate their achievement, the classic American story of small-town tinkerers achieving a dream that had fascinated people since prehistory. However factual the Wrights' achievement was, the meanings we have attached to it go much further.

As for Whitehead, he is hardly the household word that the Wrights are. But to the people who accept his claim—many of them in Connecticut, where his flight is said to have taken place—his achievement, too, has a mythic quality, inspiring them to dispute the Wrights' claim, marshal evidence on Whitehead's behalf, and spread the dramatic story of a man whose achievement was ignored for more than a century. Indeed, the Connecticut State Legislature recently proclaimed Whitehead's achievement as The First Flyer.[2] One can easily imagine, if Whitehead's claims begin to win more adherents, that we would see a concerted push to rewrite the history books, unseat the Wrights from their lofty position, and establish a new First Flight memorial in Bridgeport.

Are the events that did or did not happen in Connecticut in 1901 and in North Carolina in 1903 themselves myths? No, it is our interpretation of them—the meanings we attach to them—that makes them myths. Looked at it in this way, the whole world past and present, and the structures and substructures that we have come to identify, name (and mythologize!) are all myths we make from our own complex experiences and existences.

The Myth of Flight Reaches the Hudson

In 1909, the Hudson River Celebration Committee was planning to honor Henry Hudson's discovery of the Hudson River, and Robert Fulton's invention of the steamboat. Inspired, as everyone of that era was, by the drama of the Wright Brothers' flight in 1903, they sought to link two earlier American myths, discovery (the Hudson) and technology (the steamboat), with the most exciting event of their lifetimes. Accordingly, they contracted Wilbur Wright to fly around Governor's Island to demonstrate the new science of flight. Glenn Curtiss agreed to join the party, and both flew briefly on September 29, but Curtiss quit because of the wind. Later that day, Wright flew over the RMS *Lusitania*, which was on show at the Celebration, and then flew around the Statue of Liberty. On another day he flew to Grant's Tomb and back, allowing some million New Yorkers to see their first airplane flight.

Later that same year, New York City's *New York World* newspaper put up a $10,000 prize for the first flight from Albany to New York City. Glenn Curtiss began the 156-mile flight in his aeroplane, later to be titled the *Albany Flyer*, on May 29, 1910. And this is where Dutchess County comes into the picture: Curtiss landed at Gill Farm about halfway down the Hudson, where the IBM plant is today, and then went on to New York City to win the prize. The late Johnny Miller, a local boy who would become a well-known aviator, went over as a boy of four and a half to see all this happening. He assisted Curtiss in refueling his aircraft, and he became fixated on airplanes, altering his life forever. (He died in 2008, at the age of 102.) Miller later observed that Curtiss had been the first man to fly the Hudson River, but did it lengthwise! Much later, exactly 50 years later, on May 29, 1959, Peter Bowers flew a reproduction of the *Albany Flyer*, and flew the same flight again, but he took a little less time because he had access to a gas station, while Curtiss himself had had to rely on the help of a motorist, and Johnny Miller as well!

Figure 3: *Glenn Curtiss, a pioneer aviator, making a landing in a field at Poughkeepsie, New York, while flying the length of the Hudson River, May 1910. Curtiss was piloting his* Albany Flyer. *In this image, Curtiss is landing at Gill Farm, alongside the Hudson River, where the IBM plant is today. Photograph. Collection of Leonard E. Opdycke.*

Johnny Miller remembered seeing only a few aircraft until the start of WWI, when occasionally one came up from Long Island to help with a war-bond drive, but they only passed overhead on their way somewhere else. In 1913 Johnny did watch an airplane being assembled at Kingwood Park when the Park was opened for residential use; it arrived on a freight car in boxes and was put together and flown briefly. After the war, a barnstorming pilot arrived with his airplane, and Johnny worked with him as an unpaid mechanic. Finally the pilot moved on, leaving Johnny with his airplane and saying he could keep it if he would repair it.

Many flights later, accompanied by a growing number of fellow pilots and mechanics, Miller himself had advanced and took over the new airport in Red Oaks Mill, which Mayor Segue had opened in 1927. It was known as the Spackenkill Airport and sometimes referred to as the Poughkeepsie Airport. Miller recalled that the best customers were bootleggers, who often flew in with their goods and in so doing damaged many of their aircraft. Miller also recalled it was very hard to make money in the early years of the Depression, but the bootleggers' repairs kept the airport in funds until the Volstead Act was repealed in 1933, and Johnny Miller left to do barnstorming and later to join an airline.

Further to the east, the New Hackensack Airport was begun in the mid-1930s by a group of flyers who used it themselves. Then in the late 1930s the Civil Aeronautics Authority (CAA) began to use it and it became the official airport, renamed the Dutchess County Airport. (After WWII another airfield, known as the Arlington Airport, operated briefly on Rte 44 in what is now the Dutchess Center on Dutchess Turnpike; its activities eventually merged with those at the County Airport.)

Meanwhile, with his world-famous Old Rhinebeck Aerodrome far in the future, Cole Palen was born in 1925 in Pennsylvania, and moved with

Figure 4. *The Poughkeepsie Airport, Town of Poughkeepsie, New York, with three airplanes. Johnny Miller was running the Poughkeepsie Airport, from the early 1930s to the mid-1930s. His operation was called Giroflyers Ltd. His business made a specialty of rebuilding D-25s. The three planes in front are New Standard D-25s. 1930s. Photograph. Collection of Peter Colomello.*

Figure 5. *The interior of the Poughkeepsie Airport, Town of Poughkeepsie, New York, with men working on construction and repair of airplanes. 1930s. Photograph by Jack Ray. Collection of Peter Colomello.*

his family to a small farm in Poughkeepsie, where he grew up fascinated with airplanes, and especially with building models of them. Greatly influenced by his closeness to Spackenkill Airport, he spent a lot of time at the field, admiring the old aeroplanes and the varied aeronautical events which took place there. Just short of the end of WWII, he joined the Army, and after the war ended he entered the Aviation School on Roosevelt Field to become a mechanic. He delighted in their museum of WWI aeroplanes; after the Field and the museum closed, the aeroplanes were put up for sale and the Smithsonian Museum bought several. But Cole was so inspired by these early planes that he marshaled all of his savings and managed to outbid the Smithsonian for the last three, taking them home to store in abandoned chicken coops.

In 1959, hoping to create his own version of the Spackenkill Airport, Cole found an empty farm for sale in Rhinebeck. Making some extra money renting his WWI aircraft to the makers of the new movie *Lafayette Escadrille*, he bought the farm and built what became the start of the Old Rhinebeck Aerodrome. The first air show was in 1960, and featured not only Cole's original three aircraft, but several new acquisitions and more new reproductions. All of these planes fly regularly—weekends during the spring and summer and fall—and continue to inspire not only modelers, but builders of full-scale early aeroplanes. The author of this article built one at home from original factory drawings and flew it at Rhinebeck. It is now in a British museum hanging above the Concorde!

Figure 6. *The author's Bristol Scout N5419, built as a reproduction of a 1914 design with an original engine. The aeroplane at the Old Rhinebeck Aerodrome, 1983. Photograph by Bill Hammond. Collection of Leonard E. Opdycke.*

Conclusion

Although the histories and myths of flight and the aeroplane survive and flourish and are powerful enough to keep many dedicated people occupied with them, it is important to remember that military aircraft are central to most of the stories and events—the aeroplanes at Old Rhinebeck are mostly military. Indeed, the first markets for the first Wright and Curtiss designs were with the military, and were sold here and abroad almost exclusively for that purpose.

While for hundreds and probably thousands of years, people have noticed and been moved in many ways by the presence of birds in flight, the resulting myths all derive ultimately from our mental and physical interactions with these same experiences, including the sights and sounds of aircraft in Dutchess County.

---

[1]   Paul Jackson, "Foreword," Jane's All the World's Aircraft, March 8, 2013. In this foreword, editor-in-chief Paul Jackson reports that the Australian aviation historian John Brown, through his research, has concluded that the Bridgeport, Connecticut, engineer Gustave Whitehead flew his own design aircraft in 1901. Jackson's conclusion was: "The Wrights were right; but Whitehead was ahead."

[2]   Nina Golgowski, "Connecticut lawmakers write Wright Brother out of history as 'first in flight'," New York Daily News, June, 27, 2013. "Gov. Dannel P. Malloy signed the bill into law that names Gustave Whitehead as the first person to fly a powered airplane. The historic change is the result of newly discovered photos by aviation historian John Brown."

Poppies from Heaven 1928

By David Johnson

*This essay, submitted by Leo Opdycke, was first printed in his journal,
WW1 Aero, in 1998, and is a favorite of his. Now, in the summer of 2014,
one hundred years after those first "guns of August" were heard, heralding
the beginning of the first World War, it is fitting to look back at the events
that altered our world and started the modern era. In 1928, just ten years
after the war drew to its exhausted end with the Armistice of 1918, the
events in this article took place. The war was still manifest in peoples'
lives. This essay is included here as another approach to the concept of
"thinking historically"—in this case, with the emphasis upon a narrative,
psychological, and emotional, rather than an analytical or theoretical approach.—The Editor.*

On a cool winter's evening, subtle light blends with the warm glow of a
fireplace casting deep shadows among an array of memorabilia that adorns
a large living room.[1] Conversation with Captain Miller drifts casually from
topic to topic, guided by models of various aircraft suspended from the ceiling that drift to and fro. My thoughts recall the Air and Space Museum in
Washington, D.C., where two of the originals hang, each flown many hours
by Capt. Miller. For the last 75 years, from the Jenny to the jet, Capt. Miller has flown them all, each in its day of glory. Our attention focused on a
poster from Capt. Miller's barnstorming days during the Roaring Twenties.
"Did I ever tell you about the time poppies fell from heaven?" he asked.
"Why no," I responded, discounting all the previous times I had heard that
story. We settled back in our chairs as our minds drifted off to 1928.

Flight was still in its infancy. The airport in
Poughkeepsie, New York, was located at
Red Oaks Mill, just outside of town and
consisted of nothing more than a grass
runway that hosted a few privately owned
biplanes. On the morning of November
10, John was working diligently on minor
adjustments to the Hispano-Suiza engine

Figure 1. *Johnny Miller, November, 1932.
Photograph. Collection of Trish Taylor.*

that powered his Standard J-1 biplane. As he worked, his attention was drawn to nearby Vassar Road, where a large touring car rapidly approached, followed by a cloud of dust. The six occupants, some seated and some standing on the running boards, were dressed in various military uniforms and wearing American Legion caps. The vehicle turned onto the field, stopping abruptly alongside John so they could explain to him the urgency of their visit. The next day marked the tenth anniversary of Armistice Day, which terminated World War I. To commemorate this anniversary, a bronze plaque memorial to Poughkeepsie's war dead was to be dedicated in front of City Hall at the corner of Main and Market Streets the following day. At exactly the eleventh minute of the eleventh hour of the eleventh day of the eleventh month, "Taps" would be played as the plaque was unveiled. To accentuate the spirit of that moment, they envisioned poppies from heaven silently showering down over the participants. To accomplish such a feat, they requested John's assistance.

Figure 2. *Standard J-1 biplane with Hispano-Suiza engine originally owned by Johnny Miller in 1928 when he flew over City Hall, Poughkeepsie, New York. It is currently being rebuilt by Jim Hammond. Photo by Jim Hammond.*

The Mission

John was more than happy to accommodate them, agreeing to drop the poppies at precisely 11:11 a.m. the following morning. Relieved that their mission would be a success, they unloaded two huge bags of artificial poppies, the symbol of the American Legion's fundraising efforts and of the famous World War I poem "In Flanders Fields." ("In Flanders fields where poppies blow/Between the crosses row on row.") As they departed, John returned to his work and contemplated his upcoming mission.

The next day the mid-Hudson Valley was greeted by a clear, cold front accompanied by a light breeze from the northwest. John, never one for hasty decisions or miscalculations, had meticulously considered every aspect of his mission. The direct line distance from the airport to City Hall was just four miles which required a four-minute flight in a Standard J-1. Not to detract from this solemn occasion, a silent approach was required.

Timing was essential. An early arrival would require circling until the proper time, thus drawing attention to the plane. Tardiness would render the poppies meaningless.

Departure was set for exactly 11:05 with a northwest heading that would intersect Main Street, which then led directly to the "bombing target." During the flight, sufficient altitude would have to be achieved to permit a silent, powerless descending glide to the target, thus maintaining the element of surprise. The solemn interlude of "Taps" was not to be broken. Along the approach, Main Street ran straight and level. Beyond the memorial, Main Street sloped downhill terminating at its junction with the Hudson River. The downhill slope would compensate for the powerless descent of the aircraft, permitting a resumption of power beyond the ceremony and well out of hearing range. Once over the river, turning northwest into the wind with full throttle, altitude would be regained. John was confident his plan would succeed. He positioned the plane on the runway as his departure time neared.

In spite of John's vigilance, an old friend—Murphy's Law—now took over. A pilot friend was scheduled to arrive half an hour before departure to assist John. Ignition required more than simply throwing a switch. To safely complete this task, two people were required: one in the cockpit to adjust the throttle and work the ignition switch, the other to crank the propeller. This was complicated by the fact that it was a 9'2" left-handed Hamilton wood propeller. By 10:40, his assistant had not arrived. Since the cold engine would need several minutes to warm up, John quickly began to prepare for a hand-cranking start.

Then, just in the nick of time, an old friend happened to stop by for a visit, totally unaware of what was in store for him. Advised of the situation, Randolf agreed to help. When it came to electronics he was a wizard, but a pilot he was not, and this concerned John. Cranking the propeller and synchronizing the switch was not a job for amateurs. Chocks were placed in front of the wheels to keep the plane from a forward motion; the throttle was adjusted and the stick that operated the elevators was held in place by a seat belt so that Randolf could just stand alongside the pilot's cockpit and reach in to work the switch. As John cranked the propeller he would call out "Switch on" or "Switch off" at the appropriate times. Improper timing could result in serious injury to John. Old Reliable was ready to go: the engine had never failed John before. That is, until that moment.

John cranked and cranked and cranked until time was running out. He listened to his heart pounding rapidly from exertion as the dream of poppies from heaven faded from memory. The harder he pulled the weaker he became. Lurking beneath his sleeve his wristwatch proclaimed the time— 11:04. "One more try!" Mustering forth the last of his strength he executed the weakest cranking motion thus far. To their surprise the engine started.

Now the scramble was on. Randolf hurriedly climbed into the front cockpit and tucked himself in with the box of poppies. John raced through a short but formidable obstacle course to complete the task at hand. Diving behind the revolving propeller he pulled away the chocks. Rolling under the wing, he leaped into the rear cockpit and took command of the controls.

There was no time for proper procedures. Warm-up, magneto check, and safety belt adjustment would be accomplished in flight.

Opening the throttle on an ice-cold, water-cooled engine yielded little response. The engine burped, snorted, pounded, and back-fired as the plane slowly accelerated down the grassy runway. The row of trees marking the end of the runway grew taller and taller. At the last possible moment, John pumped the throttle and pulled back on the stick, allowing a moment of relief as the plane slipped over the tallest trees. Now nothing stood between them and their objective except a sputtering engine.

Turning right to 330 ft. he began a shallow climb with intermittent bursts of power from the cold engine, sounding like a bad case of the hiccups. Neither John nor Randolf had time to enjoy the scenery, for they were mesmerized by the irregular spinning of the propeller driven by some of the eight cylinders.

The Flight

By the time they had intersected Main Street they had reached only 400 ft., barely enough to execute the mission. Converging lines of store fronts, parked automobiles, and trolley cables pointed the way to their objective a half mile away. John aimed a fast pass directly for the drop zone. Throttling back reduced engine clamor, but with each passing moment John's pessimism grew stronger. Having no time to look at his watch, he was certain that he would be too late for the playing of "Taps." Without power, the propeller windmilled in the rush of air passing by. John pumped the throttle to keep the engine going until it could re-warm itself and blow out any ice build-up within the carburetor. Without carburetor heat, ice was removed by backfiring. At the same time an unscheduled landing site had to be determined. The trolley wires were simply unacceptable, let alone the dock at the end of Main Street which supported a large thick wooden barrier that prevented runaway trolley cars from exiting Main Street into the Hudson River. John picked a point in the river where he hoped to dunk the plane provided he could not clear the barrier. Randolf was no aviator, but no one had to tell him the dock was too close for comfort as he sank further and further into the passenger cockpit.

The silence was broken only by the whistling of the brace wires on the wing.

As the target site neared, they were surprised to see an enormous milling crowd in the intersection in front of City Hall and flowing out into the cross streets. Gliding silently over the ceremony at an altitude of only 250', they had no way of knowing how far the program had progressed. Randolf impatiently waited for John's command with the box of poppies positioned on his lap. By now John had become increasingly concerned with their descending altitude. The trolley cables were dangerously close. Hastily estimating his position, John yelled, "Now!" Randolf dumped the poppies over the right side. Momentarily glancing back they were amazed to see a huge cloud formed by what seemed to be at least 10,000 poppies descending on the crowd.

Descent to the River

John's attention was quickly caught up in the emergency at hand. Precariously they glided at an altitude of less than 250' while paralleling Main Street's descent to the river. John waited until one block beyond the drop site before opening the throttle. The engine banged, sputtered and snorted but provided precious little power. The engine, which had never really warmed up on the short flight from the airport, had lost what little heat it had had during the silent glide to the target.

Figure 3. *View of the Poughkeepsie Waterfront at the end of Main Street. (showing the Hudson Valley Bridge [built 1930] and the Railroad Bridge [1889], the trolley, the ferry, and ferry dock, as well as a number of other buildings, and the Hudson River).*

John's and Randolf's eyes opened wider and wider as the trolley wires grew closer and closer. Both being knowledgeable about electricity, they realized the wires carried 600 volts. To land on them would culminate in a spectacular display of fireworks, in which they would be unwilling participants.

In a moment it was over. They cleared the dock and leveled out over the water with intermittent power. Now, blessed with ground-effect, they bought precious time gliding just a few feet above the river as the air cushioned between the plane and the water provided some badly needed lift. John, having a long standing love affair with his airplane, was determined to stay out of the water. Randolf was deeply grateful for that. Both men felt as though "their hearts were in their throats" with teeth marks. Excitement coupled with euphoria as all eight cylinders began to run simultaneously.

A shallow right turn into a northwest breeze began a slight climb as they passed under the iron-work of the Poughkeepsie railroad bridge which towered over them. After a mile or two, they gained power and altitude sufficient for the trip home. Once on the ground, John was elated he hadn't lost his airplane while Randolf was elated he hadn't widowed his wife. They were both disappointed that they had missed the sounding of "Taps."

Within minutes they arrived back at the airport. As Randolf departed for home to hug his wife, John took some badly needed time to relax. After a while, as he expected, his attention was once again drawn to Vassar Road and a rapidly approaching touring car loaded with Legionnaires. Ready to face their flagrant criticisms, John stood prepared to meet his fate. The car slid to a stop in a cloud of dust. All four doors swung open as several

Photographic montage composed of four photographs set side by side. c. 1930–1935.
Collection of the Dutchess County Historical Society. Gift of Rebecca Curtis.

Legionnaires burst out and ran towards John. He braced for the worst as they converged at the edge of the runway.

Rallying around him, they shook his hands and slapped his back while everyone talked and laughed at once, enthusiastically thanking him for one of the most memorable moments of their lives. They went on to explain how with the passing of each note of "Taps" their hearts had sunk with the absence of the poppies. Then just as the final notes were sounding a huge cloud of thousands of poppies descended as if from heaven, a complete surprise thanks to John's silent glide. The synchronization of "Taps," unveiling of the plaque and poppies falling from heaven had led to an emotional high, bringing thousands of participants to tears. While congratulating John for his skill as a pilot, little did they know how close they came to having more than poppies fall from heaven that day.

---

[1]   Originally published as David Johnson, "Poppies from Heaven 1928," *WW1 Aero, no. 161*, August 1998, and re-published here with the author's permission. Leo Opdycke was the editor of WW1 Aero from 1961 to 2007. He is the author of "Watching Aviation in Dutchess County: Myth and Meaning, and Meaning and Myth," also in this issue. He has observed that "as we continue to think of World War I and to write the history of it, and to work on and from our myths of it, we derive much. For example, here in Dutchess County, we have the Old Rhinebeck Aerodrome" (from an interview with editor, C. Lewis, May, 2014). David Johnson, author of this essay, is an author, photographer, and educator who, in the 1990s, was working in southern Peru on geology and hydrology as well as the Lines of Nazca.

Photographs as Place Makers of the Urban Landscape: Poughkeepsie's Downtown

By Harvey K. Flad

Photographs locate people and places in space and time. Historical views of urban spaces show the city as organic, with its social and economic landscape constantly changing. They are visual texts that can be read to examine the ever-evolving character of an urban place. The Dutchess County Historical Society's collection of photographs of the City of Poughkeepsie presents a vibrant series of images of neighborhoods and commercial centers, private and public spaces, over a century and a half.

Throughout history, a city's downtown has been the locus of its civic identity. For example, as one visualizes many of the world's most famous cities, spatial images, whether linear or more concentrated, are the place makers that create meaning. In America, for both large and small cities as well as small towns, the image of its main street is a metaphor for its role in the history of a people and their lives. As my colleague social historian Clyde Griffen and I describe in *Main Street to Mainframes: Landscape and Social Change in Poughkeepsie,* "Main Street as a metaphor for a community's identity depends on a visible streetscape of social relations, a cityscape where a community can recall its past, orient itself to the present, and imagine its future."[1] Photographs of Poughkeepsie's Main Street are especially useful in depicting that history.

Poughkeepsie's origins begin in the seventeenth and eighteenth centuries on the Hudson River waterfront at the mouth of the Fall Kill and uphill at the intersection of the Albany Post Road (now Market Street) and Main Street. Commercial businesses rose along Main Street east into the town, where, as Filkintown Road, it headed east towards the farmlands of central and eastern Dutchess County and western Connecticut. Numerous industries were concentrated along the Fall Kill, the waterfront, and the northern outskirts of the city, located along lines of transportation including the docks and railroad lines. Main and Market streets constituted the central business district where primary urban functions of government, finance, and commerce were located.

Commerce symbolized the settlement pattern of mid-nineteenth century America. If the village green and white painted church and steeple symbolized "community" in pre-industrial eighteenth-century New England, the shops, banks and law offices on Main Street in eastern states and the middle west signified a bustling mid-nineteenth century industrial city.[2] During this time Poughkeepsie's population grew dramatically as factories and housing expanded, but business continued to be concentrated on Main Street.[3]

An 1863 photograph of three shops along the south side of Poughkeepsie's Main Street (Figure 1) opens a window onto the ordinary activities of a small city in the period of the Civil War: shopkeepers standing in the doorways of their shops, some of whom would live upstairs on the second or third floors, although above the shops on the left of the photograph are Miss Doughty's sewing rooms.

Women worked in the garment trades, often in factories throughout the city, while a number of individual entrepreneurs, including widows and single women, sewed dresses and hats in millineries along the main com-

Figure 1. *Shops on the south side of Main Street with Lockwood House, Poughkeepsie, NY. c.1863. Photograph. Collection of the Dutchess County Historical Society, DCPH 561B.*

mercial avenue. For example, two-thirds of the 33 dressmakers listed in the 1859 City Directory were listed as "Miss," and fifteen of seventeen milliners had addresses on Main Street. The city's growth after the Civil War led to a doubling of dressmakers, located throughout the city as well as on Main Street, along with 34 of 41 millinery and fancy and dry goods shops. Women would also be employed as clerks in the department stores and women's dress shops as Main Street commerce grew in the early twentieth century.

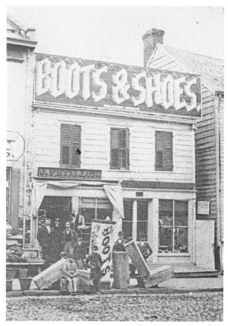

Figure 2. *Boots and Shoes, Poughkeepsie, NY. Late 19th century. Photograph. Collection of the Dutchess County Historical Society, DCPH 310.*

Signs promoted not only the products available in the shop, but also the local owner's name, as identified in Van Keuren & Bros. jewelry shop (292 Main Street) and S. Shultz boots and shoes (290 Main Street). (Figure 1) Sometimes, the sign indicating what is sold in the shop is much larger than the name of the proprietor, as in the photograph "Boots and Shoes." (Figure 2) In this photograph, the store's sign overwhelms the proprietor and clerks below; it is new and bold, replacing the earlier one now discarded on the sidewalk below. Dramatic and massive, it is a predecessor of billboards that will litter the roads and highways of America in the following century when the population takes to the wheel. In the twentieth century the automobile will tear the hearts out of city downtowns while taking their commerce with them to shopping centers and malls. A close reading of "Boots and Shoes" offers the viewer a glimpse into the past as well as a key to interpreting the auto-centered landscape of the future.

A photograph of Main Street from 1869 (Figure 3) also combines the past with intimations of the future. The photograph focuses on a street clock as it places the cobblestone street and wood framed and brick buildings into the background. Time and space, the photographer asks, which will control?

Figure 3. *Main Street, Poughkeepsie. 1869. Photograph. Collection of the Dutchess County Historical Society, DCPH 361.*

During the nineteenth century the time clock in the factory had begun to control workers' lives. By 1883, the continent would be divided into time zones so that trains could keep their schedules. Before that, localities kept their own local or solar time, usually agreed to from a clock centrally located and visible to the whole community, like the street clock in the photograph. It is on Main Street, the center of the city's business. Standard time was adopted in 1918. Modernity required temporal organization such as railroad timetables and punch clocks at work places.

In a late nineteenth century view of Poughkeepsie's Main Street (Figure 4), the thoroughfare is projected as the thread that ties the entire cityscape into one organic whole. Three and four storey buildings project an image of downtown as the core of social and commercial activity, as the shops under their canopies seem to hum with activity. Main Street is the artery that carries the blood of the urban system with its transportation network of horses and wagons, trolley tracks, and telegraph lines.

 Poughkeepsie's horse-drawn trolleys began shortly after the Civil War era photographs of cobblestone streets and horses and wagons. The city had its telephone and telegraph system installed by 1880, thus offering a glimpse into the post-bellum growth of technology in America.[4] In 1894 the trolley was electrified and ran from the Main Street dock at the steamboat landing on the Hudson River east up Main Street to Vassar College in Arlington.[5] Other routes circled the south side neighborhoods, and ran north to the Hudson River Psychiatric Hospital campus or the train station at the railroad bridge. Passengers could hop on another trolley to go to New Paltz or, if they were Vassar "girls" on an outing, to Mohonk Mountain House. The trolley even extended outside the city limits, as the aptly named Pough-keepsie City and Wappingers Falls Electric Railway ran south along South Road from Poughkeepsie's downtown to Wappingers Falls. The shops on Main Street drew in customers from near and far.

Figure 4. *A bird's eye view of Main Street looking to the west, towards the Hudson River, Poughkeepsie. c. 1890–1900. Photograph. Collection of the Dutchess County Historical Society, DCPH 717.*

So did the saloons. In the late nineteenth century photograph of Flana-gans' saloon (Figure 5) we enter into the social history of Main Street. Similar to other east coast cities like New York and Boston, Poughkeepsie grew in the mid-nineteenth century, with Irish and German immigrants joining its expanding workforce. Potato famine in Ireland and civil unrest in continental Europe forced thousands to migrate to America. In Pough-keepsie the immigrants settled in neighborhoods on the lower slope close to the waterfront and the Fall Kill. Small shops sprang up along streets sprinkled among the tenements and boarding houses, and especially along lower Main Street and the trolley line. Emblematic of this social mixture, the Irish proprietor of Flanagans' saloon sold a German-style pilsner beer.

In American history, drinking establishments were private spaces where public actions often took place. In the photograph, the swinging doors of Flanagans' saloon connected the viewer to the social meaning of the place. Saloons have a storied history in the American Imagination. They serve as an iconic image of the frontier West, but they were also a signature component of working-class and immigrant urban neighborhoods in the rest of country, especially in cities where the drinking water was of poor quality and alcoholic beverages like beer could be a healthier substitute. Many tenements and boarding houses on lower Main Street had unsanitary facilities such as outhouses and limited access to clean water.[6] There were 68 saloons in Poughkeepsie in 1890 in a city of only 22,000; sixty percent were located in neighborhoods in the lower slope wards, one-third of which were on lower Main Street between the waterfront and Market Street.[7]

Figure 5. *Flanagan's Saloon, Main Street, Poughkeepsie. 1890. Photograph. Collection of the Dutchess County Historical Society.*

The number of drinking establishments remained high throughout the early twentieth century. For example, during the Prohibition era, Poughkeepsie artist (and "cartographer extraordinary") Tom Barrett located a half dozen "Speakeasies" on his 1931 map of Poughkeepsie.[8] They are all on the lower slope, among the private residences and rooming-houses of the Irish and Germans, as well as the Italians, Polish and other immigrants that had arrived in the city in the late nineteenth and early twentieth centuries. Barrett's "Speakeasy" locations were both "formal" and "informal" and included those with frontage on Main Street, while locations of where one could purchase ravioli or spaghetti in the Mount Carmel area indicate the evolving demographics of urban communities as Italian families moved into the formerly Irish neighborhood.

Behind many of the shops fronting on Main Street, like Flanagans' in the late nineteenth century, were stables and farmers' sheds for the horses and wagons, like the one in front of Miss Doughty's Sewing Rooms (Figure 6). These arrived in the city from the surrounding countryside carrying goods and produce to be shipped south to urban markets by river and rail. For example, Erts Brothers stables and farmers' sheds were located in the rear between Flanagans' saloon and Daniel R. Spratt's drug store in 1897 (Figure 5). Meanwhile, the trolley, whose tracks are in the photograph's foreground, ran the length of Main Street (bird's eye view, Figure 4) to the Main Street dock.

Although the Poughkeepsie trolley ceased operation in 1935, the tracks remained for another decade as seen in the 1944 photograph of Main Street (Figure 7). By the World War II period, busses had taken over urban transit, although the private automobile would soon command space on Main Street. Downtown thrived in the post-war era and shopping on Main Street is still recalled by many as an anticipated event, the time when one "dressed up." Poughkeepsie's downtown drew shoppers from throughout Dutchess County with signs noting the mileage to Luckey, Platt's department store on highways eastward to the Connecticut state line. In the photograph of Main Street just east of the intersection with Catherine Street and Academy Street the street beckons shoppers to park and enter its shops. For example, Eleanor Roosevelt drove from Hyde Park and was often seen shopping at the Mohican Market, seen on the left, on the north side of the street. Across the street, the French Bakery enticed with its pastries, while many other shops, both local and national, vied for customers.

Figure 6. *Straw hats for sale in the display window of Van Kleeck's Men's Store on Main Street, Poughkeepsie. 1924. Photograph. Collection of the Dutchess County Historical Society, DCPH 707.*

A 1924 photograph of the storefront window of Van Kleeck's men's furnishing store showcases the classic straw hat of the 1920s (Figure 6). This image collapses both time and space as the Roaring Twenties arrived in Poughkeepsie at the oldest locally owned shop in the city. Van Kleeck's opened in 1799 and upon closing in 1960 was possibly the nation's oldest retail business carried on under the same family.

Locally owned shops sold everything from shoes and stationery to furniture and flowers. Dozens of women's clothing shops, such as Kay's, Mayflower, and the Town Shop (seen in the 1944 photograph, Figure 7) vied with Up-to-Date for the finest fashions, while businessmen went across the street to M. Schwartz & Co. or Wallace's. Mothers shopping for children went further east up Main Street to Effron's Young Folks shop. Luckey, Platt & Co. was a full department store with men's and women's furnishings as well as children's departments.

Figure 7. *View of Main Street with women's shops: Kay's, Mayflower, and the Town Shop, Poughkeepsie. 1944. Photograph. Collection of the Dutchess County Historical Society.*

The many stores selling similar items allowed for competition; sales were frequent among furniture stores such as Perlmuter's and Sherman's, or shoe stores such as Friedman's, Warshaw, A.S. Beck, and French Boot, or Doff's for children's shoes. Services as well as goods were available along Main Street, such as photography at Arax and State Studios; electronics at Rocket Stores; luggage at Cedar's; greeting cards and party goods at House of Cards, McComb's, or Celebrate; drugs at various pharmacies such as City Drug or Whelan's; and dozens of optometrists, dentists, and legal services, many of which were on the second floors.

Figure 8. *View of Main Street, Poughkeepsie. 1956. Photograph. Collection of the Dutchess County Historical Society.*

A photograph of Main Street in the 1950s (Figure 8) provides insight into both the modernization and nationalization of American retail businesses. Both S.S. Kresge and W.T. Grant were national chain stores, while A.S. Beck had other regional outlets. Kresge, Grant, Sears, Ward's, and Woolworths were prominent on the main streets of America, but would soon move out to suburban shopping centers as suburbanization sucked the economic heart out of downtowns.

Automobiles clogged Main Street as shoppers vied for parking spaces. Poughkeepsie attempted to alleviate the crunch by installing parking meters (foreground Figure 8). Meanwhile, shopping plazas and later malls were built outside city centers with massive parking lots for the suburban shoppers. In an attempt to stop the bleeding of retail space and sales taxes from Poughkeepsie's downtown, the city undertook urban renewal projects that cleared properties for parking lots and installed a pedestrian mall in place of Main Street. Traffic left with the construction of two one-way arterials through the city. Activity in the downtown decreased significantly and locally owned stores followed the national chains outside the city; for example, Up-to-Date, De's Jewelers, and Cedar's Luggage all relocated to Poughkeepsie Plaza on Route 9 in the town.

Reopening of Main Street in 2001 has restored activity to downtown Poughkeepsie. Many of the buildings shown in the nineteenth-century photographs have vanished due to urban renewal; for example, the site of Flanagans' saloon (Figure 5) is now the location of the building housing the Chamber of Commerce. However, the streetscape of the forties and fifties (Figures 7 and 8) is remarkably intact.

An examination of historic photographs of Main Street suggests how the evolution of the streetscape offers a window into the social, economic, and spatial changes that have occurred over a century and a half in Poughkeepsie, and by extension, to the downtowns of America's cities.

---

[1] Harvey K. Flad and Clyde Griffen, *Main Street to Mainframes: Landscape and Social Change in Poughkeepsie* (Albany: The State University of New York Press, 2009), p. 3.

[2] For a description of the nineteenth-century Main Street as "symbolic," see D. W. Meinig, "Symbolic Landscapes: Some Idealizations of American Communities," *The Interpretation of Ordinary Landscapes: Geographical Essays*, edited by D.W. Meinig (New York: Oxford University Press, 1979), pp. 164–92.

[3] For a history of the growth of Poughkeepsie's Main Street business, especially in the nineteenth century, see Edmund Platt, *The Eagle's History of Poughkeepsie* (Poughkeepsie NY: Platt & Platt, 1905; repr. Poughkeepsie, NY: Dutchess County Historical Society, 1987).

[4] The relationship of urban infrastructure development to central business districts is described by numerous historians and geographers, including Robert M. Fogelson, *Downtown: Its Rise and Fall, 1880–1950* (New Haven, CT: Yale University Press, 2001) and Edward K. Muller, "Building American cityscapes," in *The Making of the American Landscape*, 2nd ed., ed. Michael P. Conzen (New York: Routledge, 2010), pp. 303–28; for Poughkeepsie, see Platt, *Eagle's History* and Flad and Griffen, *Main Street to Mainframes*, especially pp. 68–73.

[5] For a description of the trolley ride from the steamboat dock to Vassar College in 1932, see Francis Goldsmith, "Poughkeepsie Trolley Ride" (5-page MS, April 1956) in the Adriance Memorial Library Local History Room; the range and history of Poughkeepsie's trolley system is in Flad and Griffen, *Main Street to Mainframes*, pp. 64–68.

[6] Helen Thompson, *A Report of a Housing Survey in the City of Poughkeepsie* (Poughkeepsie, NY, 1919).

[7] Author's analysis of street addresses of all saloons listed in *Le Roy's City Directory* (Poughkeepsie, NY: 1890).

[8] T. Barrett, "A Map of Poughkeepsie, 1931" (Poughkeepsie, NY: Dutchess County Art Association, reprint edition, 1977).

How Poughkeepsie Contributed to the Enlistment of Blacks in the Union Army

by Julia Hotton

In this essay, the author has addressed the theme of "thinking historically" by presenting a picture of a critically important period in our national story and then finding a local narrative of compelling interest. Dr. Hotton's thesis pivots on a barely known convention held in Poughkeepsie, New York during the Civil War and the almost completely forgotten document that recorded it.—Editor

From the onset of the Civil War, free black people throughout the country expressed a wish to join the Union Army in order to help in the eradication of slavery. The Government, however, did not accept their offer to serve. During the early stage of the war, President Lincoln opposed black recruitment, doubting the ability of blacks to be effective soldiers. He also made it clear that his objective was to restore the Union, not to save or destroy slavery; but at the same time Lincoln expressed his personal wish that all men everywhere could be free.[1]

In spite of the Union's stance against black enlistment during the early stage of the conflict, black people continued to strive for meaningful involvement in the war by urging the emancipation and use of the large slave population. One of the most eloquent and outspoken proponents on the subject was former slave and avid abolitionist, Frederick Douglass. At the beginning of the war, Douglass pleaded with the government to free the slaves as a war measure and recruit them into the Union Army. He used every opportunity to promote this idea; in editorials, speeches, letters, and interviews, he was unrelenting. In one of his articles Douglass reasoned that freeing the slaves would "smite the rebellion in the very seat of its life,"[2] depriving it of the labor which kept the rebel army supplied with food, clothing and the essentials of war.

President Abraham Lincoln's Emancipation Proclamation

January 1, 1863

As the war ground on, unexpected events began to reshape Lincoln's attitude about the use of blacks in the military. Some members of Congress began to advocate for black enlistments, while a few local commanders began to form black units on their own. These quietly organized black units consisted of the First South Carolina Regiment, the First and Second Regiment of Kansas Volunteers, and the First Regiment Louisiana Native Guards. That these regiments performed admirably and helped to ease manpower shortages in the areas where they were formed, made a positive impression on the President.[3] It was also evident that the labor of thousands of fugitive slaves who were escaping to Union lines for protection, was indispensable to the Union efforts. The contrabands (the escapees were called contraband of war), performed much needed work such as building forts, roads, and bridges and foraging for food for the troops. These former slaves had an unrivaled knowledge of the South's waterways and land configurations and were said to be the greatest single source of military and naval intelligence for the Union during the war. Contrabands were an acknowledged effective military and naval resource who willingly and enthusiastically served the Union cause, proving that they could adapt to a free labor economy, and that no sacrifice was too great be free.[4]

These and other events, no doubt, influenced Lincoln's thinking about how emancipation and the enlistment of blacks might be an effective war strategy. In the summer of 1862, Lincoln informed his cabinet of his plan to issue a proclamation, on January 1, 1863, to emancipate slaves in those states that remained in rebellion. In September of 1862, Lincoln officially announced his intention to issue a Proclamation of Emancipation on January 1, if by that time the rebel states had not laid down their arms.[5]

Elated blacks and abolitionists waited with bated breath, hoping that nothing would happen to change the President's extraordinary plan before January 1. Lincoln must have felt secure about including the black enlistment as part of the proclamation sensing that Northern public opinion on the subject was quickly changing. Many governors who were finding it difficult to raise their quotas of troops began to see the enlistment of blacks as a solution to the problem. The scores of Northern families who were suffering extensive losses began to see the advantage of black enlistment. One Union Chaplain noted: "We needed that the vast tide of death should roll by our own doors, and sweep away our fathers and sons, before we could come to our senses and give the black man the one boon he was asking for so long – permission to fight for our common country."[6]

In many ways the Congress was ahead of Lincoln in recognition of the importance of the enslaved population to the war effort. Their passage of the Confiscation Act enabled fugitive slaves, escaping military labor with the Confederate army, to take flight into Union lines for protection of the Union Army. They later adopted the articles of war that forbade military personnel to return fugitive slaves to their owners. This action resulted in fugitive slaves fleeing to Union lines in unprecedented numbers. Soon after that, Congress passed a Second Confiscation Act that declared free all slaves whose owners supported the rebellion. They even authorized the enlistment of "persons of African descent" into the military.[7] The last two acts were passed over Lincoln's objections. While legal, they did not have the support of the administration's war department until the issuance of the Emancipation Proclamation. The mood in Congress may have been best expressed in a letter from Senator John Sherman to his older brother, William Tecumseh Sherman in August:

> You can form no conception at the change of opinion here on the Negro question. Men of all parties who now appreciate the magnitude of the contest and who are determined to preserve the unity of the government at all hazards, agree that we must seek and make it the interests of the Negros to help us.[8]

When the long awaited day came, and the edict was issued, it did indeed contain the following words soliciting help of the Negro:

> …such persons (emancipated slaves) of suitable condition will be received into the armed service of the United States to garrison forts, positions, stations and other places, and to man vessels of all sorts in said service.[9]

The challenge now was the recruitment of blacks in the numbers promised by abolitionists like Frederick Douglass. It was up to the Governors of the States loyal to the Union to begin the process. John A. Andrew, Governor of Massachusetts, was the first to request permission to raise two regiments of Negro troops to serve for three years. When permission was granted by the War Department, Governor Andrew announced the formation of the 54th Massachusetts regiment, the first black regiment to be recruited in the North.

Because the black population in Massachusetts was relatively small, the Governor's appointee in charge of black recruitment set up recruiting posts from Boston to St. Louis with Negro leaders to act as recruiting agents. Frederick Douglass was personally solicited as an agent. He was thrilled to join the effort. Within days of his agreeing to become an agent for Massachusetts, Douglass issued his famous call:

Men of Color, To Arms

From East to West, from North to South, the sky is written all over, NOW OR NEVER. Liberty won by white men would lose half its luster. Who would be free themselves must strike the first blow. Better even die free, than to live slaves.[10]

The recruiting agents accomplished their tasks so well, providing more than enough men to fill the quota of the Fifty-fourth. There were enough volunteers to develop another regiment, the Massachusetts Fifty-fifth. Other states soon followed: Rhode Island with the first colored artillery regiment in the North, and Pennsylvania with ten full regiments, one of which, the Third United States Regiment, was in front of Fort Wagner when it surrendered.[11]

Horatio Seymour, the Governor of New York State

New York State was another matter. When Democratic Governor, Horatio Seymour showed no interest in raising black troops in the state, a committee of prominent New Yorkers managed to get a meeting with President Lincoln to find out what the government might do to assist in the matter. While Lincoln was impressed with the fact that the delegates already had over 3,000 pledges and the potential for 7,000 more Negroes for enlistment from the state, he told them that it was still up to the Governor of the state to sign them up. The President said that the national government could not act unless Governor Seymour specifically refused to do so. Upon the return of the delegation a formal request was sent to the Governor on July 9, 1863.[12]

The Poughkeepsie Convention

While the committee and interested parties throughout the state awaited the Governor's response, a group of prominent black citizens held a convention in Poughkeepsie on July 15 and 16 to "show the government and the people their willingness to aid in the suppression of the rebellion, by organizing a large force of Colored Volunteers for the war." The call for the meeting was addressed to the Colored Citizens of the State of New York, assembled in Poughkeepsie at 10 a.m., on July 16, 1863. The Rev. J.W.C. Pennington of Poughkeepsie was elected the Convention's President. There was a Position Paper exploring the meaning of the war to blacks in particular and to all Americans in general, followed by a list of resolutions in which a variety of salient points were presented. "It is a battle for the right of self-government, true Democracy and just Republicanism, and righteous principals against anarchy, misrule, barbarism, human slavery, despotism and wrong," it declared, then continued with the reason for the meeting in the following manner:

> This contest is one in which every son and daughter of the land is, and of necessity must be, interested. It is the bounden duty of us all....all in whom the warm blood leaps, all who feel what a terrible thing is HUMAN SLAVERY – to up and struggle for God and Right.

After a series of colorful allusions to the horrors of the war and the resulting calamity if it were lost to the "movers of the Rebellion," a list of resolutions was adopted. They included reasons for joining in the fight, such as:

> Resolved, that we, the Colored Citizens of this State, are LOYAL and TRUE to the Government; that our fortunes rise and fall with it; that we are ready, anxious and willing to demonstrate that truth and loyalty on the field of battle, or wherever else we can aid in restoring the nation to its integrity and prosperity...

The Resolutions went on to innumerate the consequences of a Rebel victory, on the one hand, and the glory that success of the Union forces would bring on the other. The tenth and final numbered resolution perhaps best summarized their feelings as follows:

> Resolved, that recent events have demonstrated that men of negro lineage hold the balance of power in this contest, and that we should prove recreant to all that constitutes manhood did we fail instantly to throw our weight for the Government, nor alone in words, but by sturdy blows. We should strike, and strike hard to win a place in history, not as vassals, but as men and heroes.....

The Convention also unanimously adopted a series of additional resolutions with recommendations and actions necessary to the success of the first ten resolutions. They included business matters such as the development of a committee structure with the task of "enrolling and organizing colored troops." As can be seen in this excerpt from the action resolutions, they remained steadfast to their original purpose:

> Colored men all over the State are called upon to enroll themselves, and cause lists of the enrolled to be made out and transmitted forthwith to the Chairman of the Control Committee. And colored females are requested to form themselves into Colored Soldiers Aid Societies all over the State.....[13]

The organizers invited Massachusetts Senator, Charles Sumner and William Whiting, Solicitor to the War Department, to speak at the Convention, no doubt, in hope of getting support from sympathetic people in high places. Although neither could attend, they both sent letters full of praise and encouragement.

End of the Impasse

As days, weeks, and even months passed, there was still no response from Governor Seymour. The committee sent him another letter, again to no avail. Finally in November a delegation went to Albany to see him, and at last got Seymour's answer, which was: "I do not deem it advisable to give such authorization, and I have therefore declined to give it." Letters were then sent to the President and to the War Department with news of the Governor's official refusal to enlist blacks in New York State. The immediate reply from the War Department said they would "grant authorization to raise colored troops whose membership would be credited to the state."[14]

In December the Association for Promoting Colored Volunteering was joined by the Union League Club of New York to facilitate the recruiting of blacks as part of New York's draft quota. Within two weeks, the quota was filled. The recruits were sent to Rikers Island for training. In March of 1864, the Twentieth United States Colored Troops left Rikers Island for Manhattan. At the foot of Thirty-sixth Street and East River, they disembarked, formed in regimental line, and with loaded muskets and fixed bayonets marched to the Union League Clubhouse where a flag presentation ceremony had been arranged. A newspaper reported the scene:

> A vast crowd of citizens of every shade of color, every phase of social and political life, filled the square and streets, and every door, window, veranda, tree and house top that commanded a view of the scene, was peopled with spectators.[15]

After the ceremonies, the soldiers enjoyed refreshments with friends and family. The troops then boarded a ship to their first assignment in New Orleans. By joining the struggle to defend the country of their birth, the brave men of the Twentieth United States Colored Troops joined with over 200,000 of their black brothers in arms to hasten the end of the rebellion, free their people, and strengthen America's values. Their valor did not go unappreciated, as can be seen in a letter General Grant wrote to President Lincoln:

> I have given the subject of arming the negro my hearty support. This with the emancipation of the negro, is the heaviest blow yet given to the Confederacy…By arming the negro we have added a powerful ally….[16]

And the President, whose change of strategy from making the sole purpose of the war to save the Union, a combined effort to free the slaves, seemed pleased with his decision. Lincoln is reported to have thought the effect of the Emancipation Proclamation had broken the backbone of the Confederacy and to have said that it was "The Central act of my administration, and the greatest event of the Nineteenth Century."[17]

---

[1] Benjamin Quarles, *The Negro in The Civil War* (New York: Da Capo Press, Inc. of Plenum Publishing Corp. Company, 233 Spring St., unabridged republication of edition published in Boston in 1953. Reprinted by arrangement with Little, Brown & Company, 1989) p. 60.

[2] Philip S. Foner, Frederick Douglass, A Biography (New York: The Citadel Press, 2010), p. 193.

[3] Eric Foner, The Fiery Trial: Abraham Lincoln and American Slavery (New York & London: W.W. Norton & Company, 2010), p. 230.

[4] Benjamin Quarles, Ibid., pp. 95-99.

[5] Eric Foner, Ibid., p. 218.

[6] Benjamin Quarles, Ibid., p. 183.

[7] Barbara J. Fields, "Who Saved the Slaves?", from Geoffrey C. Ward with Ric Burns and Ken Burns, The Civil War, An Illustrated History (New York: Alfred A. Knopf, 1990), pp. 180-81.

[8] Benjamin Quarles, Ibid., p. 158.

[9] Ibid., p. 182.

[10] Langston Hughes, Milton Meltzer, and C. Eric Lincoln, A Pictorial History of Black Americans (New York: Crown Publishers, Inc., 1956), p. 172.

[11] Philip Foner, Ibid., p. 211.

[12] Benjamin Quarles, Ibid., pp. 188-89.

[13] Record of the Action of the Convention Held at Poughkeepsie, N.Y., July 15th and 16th, 1863 , for the Purpose of Facilitating the Introduction of Colored Troops into the Service of the United States. (New York, New York, 1863). This report was found in the New York City Public Library, Schomburg Center for Research in Black Culture: Manuscripts Archives & Rare Books.

[14] Benjamin Quarles, Ibid., p. 189.

[15] Ibid., p. 191.

[16] James M. McPherson, Marching Toward Freedom, The Negro In The Civil War 1861-1865 (New York: Alfred A. Knopf, 1965), p. 104.

[17] Benjamin Quarles, Ibid., p. 182.

ARTICLES

From Above:
Poughkeepsie, New York, 1937

by Mary Kay Lombino

"I like high shots. If you are on the same level, you lose many things." [1]
–André Kertész

The Hungarian born photographer André Kertész (1894-1985) had a seventy-three-year career marked by innovation and pioneering vision. He acquired his first camera at the age of eighteen and his early images reveal a distinctive vision and talent for composition that lasted him a lifetime. After serving briefly in World War I, he returned home and began work in the stock exchange as was expected by his family, yet he found the work unbearably boring. In 1925, at age thirty, he moved to Paris to pursue his chosen path as a photojournalist. There, his work embraced the theme of the romantic outsider, but in reality he was warmly embraced by the international artistic community which included painters, sculptors, poets, and writers, as well as numerous photographers including Robert Capa, Man Ray, Henri Cartier-Bresson, and Brassaï. He became one of the most distinguished photographers of the time enjoying many exhibitions, publications, and much praise for shaping the field of photojournalism and inventing the photo essay. When in 1936, he was offered a one-year assignment to take fashion photographs for the Keystone Press Agency in New York, he decided to take the opportunity to leave the growing uncertainties of life in Europe behind.

Kertész arrived in New York by steamer from France in October of 1936, while the forces of Fascism were building in Europe and the worst days of the Great Depression were not yet over in the United States. Shortly after arriving, he became dissatisfied with his contract with Keystone and he left the company. For the next few years, while in between magazine jobs, Kertész roamed the streets looking for interesting subjects just as he had done when he arrived in Paris a decade earlier. He was drawn to subjects that revealed both the city's architectural marvels and its unwelcoming character. He was captivated by the visual geometry of the buildings and streets, by the contrast between the old and the new, and by the dizzying panoramas the city offered. The guiding principal of his art was naturalism

Figure 1. *André Kertész (American, born Hungary, 1894-1985)*, Poughkeepsie, New York, 1937. *Gelatin silver print.* © *The Estate of André Kertész / Higher Pictures.*

and it was contrary to his style and character to arrange or alter his subjects to suit his needs. Therefore, sometimes when in the streets he had to wait for something magic to happen, often setting up his camera and waiting for the action to occur.

Photography historian, Weston Naef, who knew Kertész personally during his lifetime said, "Travel was fundamental to his manner of working. His mind was charged by new places and situations. His life has truly been an odyssey for which photographs are the journal."[2] Yet upon arriving in New York, Kertész only had the rare occasion to leave Manhattan and a trip to Poughkeepsie during his first year there was one of those moments. *Poughkeepsie, New York* was taken in 1937 (Figure 1) when the artist took the train to visit a friend's home in Poughkeepsie. While he waited for his train back to New York, he was struck by the angle from above the track, and decided on a whim to create this striking image. The composition brilliantly merges the traveler's descent down the stairs and the train's expected arrival on the track. The picture is filled with anticipation, fittingly illustrated by the figure near the top, right edge of the picture, dressed in bright white with his hands on his hips, his form is braced by the sharp vertical line of the track that leads down toward the path of future travel.

Robert Gurbo's apt description of the work points out Kertész's emphasis on the personal alienation and the inhospitable aspects of urban life. He wrote,

> In *Poughkeepsie, New York*, 1937, he used all the formal lessons he had learned in   Hungary and Paris to record the complex web of modern mechanized city. He contrasted the jagged staircase descending to the

Figure 2. *André Kertész (American, born Hungary, 1894-1985),* Stairs of Montmartre, Paris, *1925. Gelatin silver print.© The Estate of André Kertész / Higher Pictures*

platform with the gleaming lines of the track and an expanse of white roof in order to create a boldly dynamic photograph of the modern city. But,

Gurbo argues,

> in *Poughkeepsie, New York* none of the people interact with each other; they look down at the platform, off to the side, or past one another. ...the architecture seems more energetic and engaged than its inhabitants.[3]

It has been speculated that this lack of human engagement was a reflection of Kertész's dissatisfaction with his life in New York. He found life in America more difficult than he had imagined, beginning a period that he later referred to as tragic. He longed for the career momentum and supportive artistic community he had enjoyed in Paris, but the progress of the War made his return to Europe impossible.

There is also the possibility that *Poughkeepsie, New York* is not a reflection of Kertész's feelings of isolation in New York, but instead a continuation of his interest in capturing the view from above, a formal strategy he began to employ while he was in Paris. Prior to coming to New York, Kertész created some of his greatest works with a similar angle, looking down on his

Figure 3. *André Kertész (American, born Hungary, 1894-1985),* Carrefour, Blois, *1930. Gelatin silver print.* © *The Estate of André Kertész / Higher Pictures.*

Figure 4. *André Kertész (American, born Hungary, 1894-1985),* Shadows of the Eiffel Tower, *1929, Gelatin silver print. © The Estate of André Kertész / Higher Pictures.*

subject. Examples include such well-known works as *Stairs of Montmartre* (1925, Figure 2), *Carrefour, Blois* (1930, Figure 3), and *Eiffel Tower, Paris* (1929, Figure 4). *Stairs of Montmartre,* made only a few months after his arrival in Paris, looks down onto the steps in a normal perspective of an observer standing at the top. Kertész scholar Sandra Phillips notes that the artist was attracted to Montmartre, with its cobblestone streets and hilly terrain, because it reminded him of Buda, the old section of his native city.[4] Looking down from the stairs is a natural viewpoint for any visitor to Montmartre yet in Kertész's image, there is an emphasis on the twisting action between vantage point and ground plane that imbues the composition with a critical, even analytical element. The pattern in the foreground created by the crossing of shadow over the steps is echoed by the repeating pattern of the cobblestones in the background. A series of diagonal lines point towards the black figure approaching from the left while the lone figure at the bottom of the stairs seems frozen in place like an axis with the rest of the image is set in motion around it.

In *Carrefour, Blois* (Figure 3), made five years later, the cobblestone pattern returns from a slightly higher angle and now paired a contrasting pattern of roof tiles. Speaking about this picture Kertész said, "There are many wonderful things between you and the horizon when you're high up. So I climbed up church towers and mountains."[5] Here we see Kertész's sensitive appreciation of light, the delicacy of his tonalities, and directness and simplicity of composition. More importantly, he employs planar tensions and geometric structure in a new way. These concerns might be seen as more formalist than his previous work perhaps owning to his appreciation for abstract paintings by such artists as Piet Mondrian, Fernand Léger, and others showing in Paris at the time.

The most well known of these three works taken from above is *Eiffel Tower, Paris* (Figure 4), which utilizes a more dramatically angled point of view. The grandeur of the architecture is made clear through the artist's attention to light's effect on its form. A few years before making this image, he had made several studies of the Eiffel Tower as a freestanding subject. This view, however, takes as its subject the shadows of the ironwork and the pedestrians at the base of the tower. While a full aerial view would certainly have been possible, Kertész chose to shoot this image from the first floor of the tower in order to capture the long shadows cast by the sun. The viewer's eye is directed not towards the human experience of the building but instead to the ornate pattern made by the people milling around below

Figure 5. *André Kertész (American, born Hungary, 1894-1985),* Distortion # 147, *1933. Gelatin silver print. © The Estate of André Kertész / Higher Pictures.*

the elaborate structure.

The similar viewpoint of these works to *Poughkeepsie, New York* is not a coincidence but the result of careful placement and framing to capture the difference in shadows of objects at varying levels from the ground. When considering other works by Kertész, it becomes evident that a different perspective on ordinary forms is central to his method and intention. A fine example of this can be found in his *Distortions*, a series of some 200 photographs made in 1933 in which he used mirrors to manipulate the female figure (Figure 5). In this series the twisted and stretched bodies of the models transcend formal concerns and show his willingness to experiment with new visual vocabularies. Looking down from above was, like the use of mirrors, a formal strategy that allowed him to take advantage of the contrasting tones produced by an oblique light source, creating dramatic silhouettes and shadows of the people and architecture present in his photographs. This innovation is one of many he achieved throughout his career and *Poughkeepsie, New York* shows that he brought his inventive spirit from Europe to the United States as he explored new territory in both the literal and the figurative sense.

---

[1]   André Kertész, *Kertész on Kertész: A Self-Portrait* (New York: Abbeville, 1985), p. 66.

[2]   Weston J. Naef, "André Kertész: The Making of an American Photographer" in *André Kertész of Paris and New York*, (New York: Thames and Hudson, 1985) p. 100.

[3]   Robert Gurbo, "The Circle of Confusion, 1936-1961," in *André Kertész* (Washington, DC: The National Gallery of Art), p. 148.

[4]   Sandra S. Phillips, "André Kertész: The Years in Paris," in *André Kertész of Paris and New York*, (New York: Thames and Hudson, 1985) p. 28.

[5]   André Kertész, *Kertész on Kertész: A Self-Portrait* (New York: Abbeville, 1985), p. 67.

Lee Miller:
Hometown Girl Does Well

by Lou Lewis

Elizabeth "Lee" Miller of Poughkeepsie has fallen off the radar for most of us. I recently had occasion to ask a half-dozen prominent local residents, all of them born and bred in Dutchess County, New York, if they knew anything about her and there were blank faces around the table. In fact, Lee Miller (1907-1977) is one of the most internationally famous people ever to come from Poughkeepsie. During the 1920s and 1930s, she was a great beauty, a Vogue model with boyish looks who personified the age of the flapper, and who, at the same time, epitomized the elegance of high fashion. Always fearless, Lee Miller decided to take up a man's profession, photography, and became a student and colleague of Man Ray, a leading member of the Surrealist Movement between World War I and World War II. In addition to becoming a Surrealist photographer and renowned portraitist, Lee Miller would have another rebirth during World War II as a war correspondent when she followed troops into Normandy and across Europe, taking photographs and writing of her experiences.

Lee Miller was born at home at 40 South Clinton Street in Poughkeepsie in 1907. Her father was superintendent at the DeLaval plant on the Hudson River (now the site awaiting development just west of Hudson Pointe). Her mother Florence was Canadian. Lee attended grade school at Governor Clinton School on Montgomery Street. In 1912, the family moved out of town to a farm known as Clinton Hill just south of Poughkeepsie. Two years or so later, the family moved again, into the home in Kingwood Park which was ceded to Lee's brother John Miller in 1944 when Lee's parents moved into an apartment in the city of Poughkeepsie. The farm was sold to IBM for $12,500 in 1944 in the belief it would help the war effort and became first the IBM Country Club and then Casperkill Golf Course. Later they moved to Kingwood Park and lived in what is now the Silver family residence there.[1]

Lee was a difficult, obstreperous child and teenager and attended a number of grade schools, high schools, and finishing schools—even taking some courses at Vassar College but not matriculating there. However, she had an expansive personality and inquiring mind in addition to great physical beauty. Her indulgent father agreed to pay for an apartment for her in New York City when she was nineteen years old. One day, she was starting to cross a busy street in Manhattan when a man behind her realized she was about to be run over by a car. He grabbed her back onto the sidewalk and they both fell over. The man was none other than the famous publisher Condé Nast and he immediately took her to his office and hired her as a fashion model for Vogue. She appeared in the pages of Vogue shortly thereafter and was soon in demand at Vogue's offices in London and Paris.[2]

Not only her beauty helped her achieve her goals, because she was possessed of a drive, sometimes seen as willfulness, that propelled her into the drama of life. In the Roaring Twenties, New York City represented that life and its possibilities far better than her hometown of Poughkeepsie. Yet her background also aided her. Lee's father Theodore had been an avid amateur photographer; Lee had been his favorite and constant subject; she was at ease in front of the camera. Success came quickly to the young Lee Miller, newly minted as a fashion model. Her image was the inspiration for

Figure 1. *Lee Miller, Self Portrait, New York Studio, New York, U.S.A., 1932. copyright Lee Miller Archives, England. All rights reserved, Negative number: 12-1-C Notes: CR.*

the cover of the spring issue of Vogue, 1927, in her first year of modeling, when she was twenty years old. It was not long, however, before Lee decided to move behind the lens. She would be quoted as saying "I'd rather take a picture than be one."[3] She became a Vogue photographer while continuing to model.

She soon sailed for France. In an effort to improve her skills and explore artistic photography as well as fashion photography, she met with the famous Surrealist photographer and artist Man Ray at his studio in Paris. Man Ray peremptorily told her that he was not taking on any apprentices and was leaving for vacation in the south of France the following day. She replied that she was coming with him and they proceeded to live together for the next three years. In the process Lee Miller became a very accomplished photographer, was involved in developing new photographic techniques, and developed her own Surrealistic oeuvre. Her invention with Man Ray of a process to which they would give the name "Solarization" is noteworthy. One day in Paris, Lee was in the darkroom developing photographs in an open pan when she felt a rat run across her foot. She screamed and turned on the white light—a forbidden activity in the darkroom which would ordinarily destroy the maturing prints. When Man Ray entered the room he was upset, but they both realized that the photographs had taken on an unusual quality with the elimination of grey tones and the appearance of a strong black line around the contours. This effect was subsequently much used in both Surrealist and fashion photography.[4]

While living with Man Ray, Lee became a friend of Pablo Picasso, Ernest Hemmingway, Max Ernst and other prominent figures of the time and photographed them. Picasso was so taken with her that he painted five or six portraits of her in French peasant costume—in his uniquely abstract style.[5]

In 1932, after returning to the United States, Lee opened a photography studio in New York City where she was in great demand by the rich and famous who wanted her to take their photographs. Film star Lillian Harvey, impresario John Housman, composer Virgil Thompson, actress Gertrude Lawrence, actor Charlie Chaplin and her discovery, the Surrealist artist Joseph Cornell all sat for her and she produced excellent, character-revealing portraits of the important personalities of her day. [6]

Upon ending her relationship with Man Ray, Lee became good friends with a man whom she would eventually marry—Roland Penrose. Penrose was a member of the landed gentry in England; he was an artist, art collector, and England's most prominent Surrealist painter. When Roland met

Lee Miller, it was at a Surrealist fancy dress ball in Paris. He was living in London at the time. However, there was much more adventure to be had before that marriage would come to pass and, in 1935, Lee found herself whisked away to Egypt on the arm of Aziz Eloui Bey, an international socialite who had fallen in love with her and convinced her to marry him. Lee was entertained for about one year with parties, picnics in the desert, and archeology.[7] She described her life there as being relegated to the "black satin and pearls" set, which was not to her taste, and spent much of her time tooting off into the desert with her camera.

She then returned to Britain just in time for The Blitz and the onset of WWII. She and her compatriots at British Vogue, or "Brogue" as they called it, frequently found themselves in air raid shelters while buildings around them were demolished. Lee was unflappable however and continued to take photographs, many now iconic, of the Brits under the stress of the bombardment.[8]

After D-Day on June 6, 1944, Lee learned that some photographers she knew were becoming war correspondents for their magazines and newspapers. Lee accredited herself as a war correspondent, completely independent of the management at British Vogue; she had a suitable uniform tailored, and without permission of anyone, went off with the United States Eighth Army to Europe just days after D-Day. She had first tried through the British Army but was refused as a female. David E. Scherman was the one who recommended she try the U.S. Army and there she succeeded. Although freelance the vast majority of the time, she published her articles in Vogue US, Vogue UK, and Vogue France.[9] At the time, women were forbidden to travel with the troops much less be at a front, but Lee soon accompanied U.S. army troops to the siege of St. Malo in Brittany. Her photographs of the explosions and bombing of that German-held fortress are amazing. She then traveled to Paris for the liberation of that city and photographed the joy of the residents there at being rescued by American troops. She took the time to seek out her friend Picasso who remarked, "This is the first Allied soldier that I have seen, and it is you!"[10]

Ignoring telegrams from British Vogue asking her to return to England, Lee proceeded to follow the fighting across Europe and into Germany. She was one of the first to enter Hitler's redoubt at Berchtesgaden and sadly, the first woman photographer to enter the camps at Dachau.[11] Her photographs of the dead and dying are both chilling and fearless. She was with American forces when they met the Russians and, of course, took many photographs and shared many bottles of vodka. [12]

As the war ended, British Vogue again pressed Lee to return to England, but instead she went on to Vienna to photograph the devastation there and in parts of Eastern Europe as well.[13] It might be said that, because of her experience with Surrealism, Lee was ideally prepared to photograph the surrealist aftermath of war. Throughout the war Lee filed dispatches with Vogue – most of which were printed in the magazine along with her photographs and later published as the book, *Lee Miller's War*. She proved to have a gift for writing as well as photography and art.[14] The period from D-Day through the next two years as Lee courageously managed to join Allied troops invading Normandy, participate in the siege of St Malo, follow the armies into Paris, then across Europe into Germany, and beyond into Eastern Europe, photographing, interviewing, writing, and publishing her work was the most vivid and trying period of her life. It was also the most brave and productive. Lee's special relationship with the ironies of life, because of her immersion in Surrealism gave her a different perspective than other photographers and writers. She seemed to have had a finely tuned appreciation of the fragility of the logic of life and, thus, could convey the madness of war .

Eventually, Lee returned to England, divorced her Egyptian husband and married Roland Penrose. Both Vogue UK and Roland pleaded with Lee to return, but it seems that David E. Scherman's telegram did the trick as he mentioned that she might lose Roland who had been waiting for her

while she had been photographing across war-torn Europe. In time Roland was recognized by the Crown for his many contributions to the arts and became Sir Roland Penrose. Lee was now Lady Penrose. They visited Poughkeepsie in the summer of 1946.[15] Roland had shipped much of his valuable art collection to Poughkeepsie for safe-keeping during the war.[16]

Figure 2. *Lee Miller in her parents' home in Poughkeepsie, NY. (With painting by Franz Marc, The Blue Horses, in background). Photograph. Collection of Trish Taylor. 1962.*

Roland Penrose and Lee bought a home together in 1949; they lived there at Farley Farm House, Muddles Green, Chiddingly, in East Sussex for the remainder of

Figure 3. *The Miller Family in 1962, from left: John, father Theodore, mother Florence, Lee. Photograph. Collection of Trish Taylor.*

their lives. At age 40, Lee had her first and only child—Antony Penrose—who has written an excellent book about his mother—*The Lives of Lee Miller*—and wrote and produced a short film about her.[17] He is now serving as Director of the Lee Miller Archives in England. Lee clearly suffered from all that she had seen and done in the war, what is known today as PTSD or post traumatic stress syndrome. In her later years, she stopped her photography altogether, became a gourmet cook and planned to publish a cook book. She wrote several articles on food and entertaining that were published. Some of the passion she had once devoted to photography she now poured into the art of cooking and homemaking. Also during these later years, Lee made some trips home to Poughkeepsie to visit her aging parents and other members of her family (Figures 2 and 3). Her niece Trish Taylor lived with her in England for a short while.[18]

Lee Miller died of cancer in 1977.[19] Instead of burial in the family plot in Rural Cemetery here in Dutchess County, she elected to be cremated and have her ashes spread on the lands of the Penrose estate in England.[20] Today Farley Farm House is the location of the Lee Miller Archives administered by her son, Antony Penrose, and the Archives staff.

[1] Trish Taylor, Lee Miller's niece, daughter of John Miller, still lives in Poughkeepsie, as does her sister. Trish adored her Aunt Lee and was the source for much of the biographical material presented here as well as two of the photographs. I interviewed her at her home in April 2014. See also Carolyn Burke, *Lee Miller -- A Life*, (New York: A Knopf Book, ebook, 2005), location 1065.

[2] Burke, Ibid, loc. 1276. See also Antony Penrose, *The Lives of Lee Miller*, (London: Thames and Hudson, 1985), pp. 16-18; Becky E. Conekin *Lee Miller in Fashion*, (New York: The Monacelli Press, 2013), pp. 22-24. There has been a significant resurgence of interest in Lee Miller and her career in the past decade or more. Carolyn Burke's *Lee Miller—A Life*, for example has been well reviewed. Ms. Burke lived in Poughkeepsie for several months with Trish Taylor while she conducted her local research. In addition to *Lee Miller in Fashion* by Becky E. Conekin of 2013, cited above, also recently published is Mark Haworth-Booth, *The Art of Lee Miller*, (New Haven: Yale University Press, 2007).

[3] Conekin, Ibid., chap. 2 and 3, for cover of Vogue, see image p. 20.

[4] Haworth-Booth, Ibid., plate 14, p. 41.

[5] Burke, Ibid., Chapter 5; Haworth, Ibid., plate 151, p. 177; Penrose, Ibid., p. 77.

[6] Burke, Ibid., loc. 2867; Haworth, Ibid., p. 53, photo at p. 54; Penrose, Ibid., p. 40.

[7] Burke, Ibid., loc. 3399; Penrose, Ibid., p. 64; Haworth, Ibid., p. 126.

[8] Burke, Ibid., chap. 11, loc. 4402; Haworth-Booth, Ibid., p.151, plate 132; p. 165, plate 142.

[9] Per private correspondence with Kerry Negahban, Lee Miller Archives, Roland Penrose Estate & The Penrose Collection, Farley Farm House, Muddles Green, Chiddingly, East Sussex BN8 6HW, England, July 14, 2014.

[10] Haworth-Booth, Ibid., p. 176, p. 177, plate 151; Burke, Ibid., loc. 4951.

[11] Haworth-Booth, Ibid., p. 163, plate 163; Burke, Ibid., loc. 5622 to 5635.

[12] Burke, Ibid., loc. 5533 to 5535,

[13] Burke, Ibid., loc. 5857 et seq.

[14] Burke, Ibid., loc. 5048, 5123, 5124.

[15] Periodically, Lee returned to Poughkeepsie to visit her father and mother and her brother John Miller. John became an airline pilot – among other things – and one of his many exploits in Dutchess County is set forth in this issue -- see "Poppies from Heaven 1928." From my interview with Trish Taylor in April, 2014.

[16] From interview with Trish Taylor .

[17] Penrose, Ibid., p. 185; see also the short film written and produced by Lee Miller's son Antony Penrose, *The Lives of Lee Miller: A Documentary by Antony Penrose: Super Model—Muse—Surrealist Photographer—Photo-journalist—Combat Photographer—Gourmet Cook*, Penrose Film Productions Ltd., Farley Farm House, Muddles Green, Chiddingly, East Sussex, BN8 6HW England. Antony Penrose's examination of his

mother's life, and the resulting book and film, were a virtual archeological search into her life, as, growing up , he had known almost nothing about her years as model, photographer, Surrealist, photo-journalist, or combat-photographer. She had not spoken of her earlier life. He did know her, however, as his mother and fabulous gourmet cook.

[18] Per interview with Trish Taylor, Ibid.

[19] Penrose, Ibid., p. 198; Burke, Ibid., loc. 7310.

[20] Per Taylor interview; Burke, Ibid, loc. 7943.

The Legacy of
Young Theodore A. Schultz
of Schultzville

by Cynthia M. Koch

The Civil War was raging and young men across the North were signing up to wear the blue uniform of the Union. Here in Dutchess County, New York, Theodore A. Schultz, a young man of military age, was unable to serve. In the midst of the war he died on January 22, 1862 after "lingering with consumption" (tuberculosis) for two years.[1] The scion of a locally prominent family in Schultzville, Town of Clinton, his father recently deceased, Theodore was the only surviving male heir in his family line.

Theodore A. Schultz lived only twenty-four years (1838–1862) but left a legacy to his community of enduring value. In his will, he bequeathed the land and monies necessary to build the meeting hall for the Masonic Warren Lodge No. 32 and the nearby First Christian (now Christian Alliance) Church and burial ground, both in Schultzville.

Theodore's father Daniel H. Schultz, had been an important member of the community, owner of several businesses. He had been one of a group of gentlemen who, in 1846, had invited a minister from the nondenominational Christian Church to preach regularly in the lecture room over his general store in Schultzville. Daniel had died in 1858 leaving young Theodore a "handsome property." Theodore was close to both the church and the Masonic Lodge. After his bequest of two-and-a-half acres and $3,000, the church was organized in 1863 and the building completed in 1866. He was described as a "devoted" member of the Lodge; his $2,000 bequest to the Masons—combined with the contributions of members—provided for the construction of the Lodge building in 1864.[2]

The Masonic Warren Lodge No. 32

The Masonic Lodge (Figure 1) was acquired by the Clinton Historical Society in 1999 and preserved and restored. Subsequently in 2011, it was sold to the Town of Clinton and moved to its present site near Town Hall, where now it houses town offices. The Masons continue to use the meeting hall on the second floor, which is also available to community groups.

Figure 1. *The Warren Masonic Lodge Number 32, Town of Clinton, Dutchess County. Photograph by Cynthia Koch.*

The second floor meeting hall is a remarkable space. Its ceiling is a barrel vault comprised of finely fitted narrow tongue-and-groove paneling that resembles the hull of a wooden ship. Within that hall, Theodore Schultz's nearly life-sized 4-1/2 x 6-1/2 foot portrait (Figure 2) has presided over the room for as long as anyone can remember—most likely since it was painted more than 150 years ago.

Figure 2. *Anonymous, Portrait of Theodore Schultz (1838-1862). Oil on canvas. Clinton Historical Society. Photograph. Clinton Historical Society.*

The Portrait of Theodore Schultz

The oil on canvas painting of young Theodore is remarkable for its large size, presumably chosen because it was going to be placed in the large public space of the Masonic Lodge. The artist, whose identity is unknown, has depicted the young man sitting on a chair in front of a stone column and red velvet curtain, facing the viewer. There is a table under his left arm (proper) and a vista showing the Hudson River over his left shoulder (proper). In his hands he holds a book and a rolled up document. He wears soft shoes, light colored trousers, a jacket, and vest. The stone column and dark red curtain had been a traditional devise at least since the grand manor English portraits of Sir Joshua Reynolds of the late eighteenth century. Objects held in the hands

Figure 3. *Anonymous, Portrait of Theodore Schultz. Detail. View of reverse with numerals "23 – 9 – 63", perhaps indicating the date of manufacture as Sep 23, 1863. Oil on canvas. Clinton Historical Society. Photograph. Clinton Historical Society.*

of the sitter or close to the sitter were usually intended to convey information about the individual's occupation: in this case, study. Theodore is shown as a quite young man, beardless—and clothed in the garments of a businessman or country squire. The setting, on the other hand, indicates neither a setting of leisure nor business, but rather projects the traditional persona of country gentleman surveying his domain. This is not to say that the painting appears pompous for it does not; it merely conforms to conventional modes of portraiture in painting. In fact, the presentation of the young man is very forthright and pleasant.

The quality of the painting, while workmanlike, is not of the highest level. The clothing, the painting style, the use of colors such as deep tones of red and green, and, naturally, the subject of Theodore Shultz all point to a date close to the time of Theodore's death in 1862.

By the fall of 2012, the Theodore Schultz portrait was much in need of conservation. The paint was cracked and flaking. It was very dirty and coming loose from its stretcher. The Clinton Historical Society, which owns the painting, hired conservator Hallie Halpern to thoroughly restore the portrait. It is unsigned and very likely dates from the early 1860s. (Handwritten "23-9-63" -- Figure 3 -- found on the back may indicate it was painted September 23, 1863.) The portrait is in its original frame and—after Ms. Halpern's work—is clean, reinforced, and consolidated. It should last another century or more. Some of Ms. Halpern's photos of the work-in-progress are seen here. When she was finished with her laborious task, which took some forty hours, the painting was rehung in the Masonic Hall where it has mostly likely hung since circa 1863 (Figure 4).

Figure 4. *Anonymous, Portrait of Theodore Schultz on the floor during installation (with installer on ladder), after conservation. Photograph. Clinton Historical Society.*

Theodore Schultz

But who was this handsome young man? In my search of old sources, I could not find much about him personally—although the mere fact that we have his portrait provides more information than we know about most Clinton residents of his time. He was obviously a young man of means; the drapery and fine furnishings, his fashionable clothing, and the very fact that his portrait was painted indicate his high social status. The view of the Hudson River in the background ties him to our region. The paleness of his complexion suggests a postmortem portrait or a portrait painted during his terminal illness. We know he was a member of the Schultz family, who were—according to William McDermott's *Clinton: A History of a Town*—among the largest landholders in the town in 1830. And we know from various historical sources that the Schultz family once owned literally all of the land in the hamlet that bears their name. Daniel H. Schultz served as postmaster of Schultzville from 1839 to 1858; the only mention of Theodore in town records is that he succeeded his father as postmaster, serving from 1858 to 1862.

The Schultz family had three or more individual heads of household listed as real estate taxpayers in 1830, with a combined total of approximately 1,300 acres for the extended family. At the time, with the exception of the Travers whose holdings were similar to the Schultzes, the ten other large landholding families owned about 400 acres each, while the median size of the farms of the remaining 165 real estate taxpaying families in Clinton was about 120 acres—basically enough to support a single farm family, but not enough to subdivide for support of the next generation.[3]

Early members of the Schultz family in this region lived on the Beekman patent in Rhinebeck as early as 1715 when, according to Hasbrouck's *History of Dutchess County*, Judge Henry Beekman offered life leases to a number of German Palatine families—including the Schultzes—to relocate from East Camp on Livingston Manor, which encompassed much of today's Columbia County.[4] The first member of the family may well have been Johannes Schiltz, listed as a ten-year-old orphan "bound to R. Livingston of Livingston Man" on January 15, 1711 according to the list, "Palatine Children Apprenticed by Gov. Hunter in New York."[5] By the end of the eighteenth century, the Schultzes were in Clinton. Frederick Schultz (1748–1819) and his wife Margaret Crapser Schultz (1754–1832) purchased land on the Crum Elbow Creek in 1788. He was an innkeeper on Schultz Hill Road in 1799 and active in town affairs as late as 1801. Frederick and Margaret were Theodore's great grandparents.[6]

Theodore's grandfather, John F. Schultz (1772–1823), erected a sawmill and gristmill in 1792 in what would become Schultzville. According to an historical pamphlet published by the Upton Lake Grange, "[John] made $100,000 out of this and passed it to his son, Daniel H. Schultz."[7] John was commissioner of highways in Clinton in first the decade of the nineteenth century and served as town supervisor in 1821–1822. He was married to Susan (1777–1827) and they are buried in the Rhinebeck Reformed Dutch Cemetery.

The Schultz family was also involved in an early industry in Clinton— quarrying slate. McDermott tells us that, in 1807, John F. Schultz purchased the quarry west of Schultzville that had first been mined in 1798. He opened a store for his workers, which also served as the town post office. An 1830 gazetteer proclaimed that the quarry "abounds in slate equal to any in the U.S. and it employed 300 hands."[8] This may well have been more boosterism than fact, for about that time problems arose concerning the quality of the slate and operations ceased.[9] It reopened under new ownership in 1866 as the Hudson River Slate Company, but, by the 1870s, closed as the mine became depleted.[10] The quarry was also associated with Schultz's Landing (or Slate Dock) on the river close to the present location of the Rhinecliff–Kingston Bridge. [11]

Theodore's father, Daniel H., was an important businessman in Clinton. In addition to the sawmill, gristmill, store, and post office, he operated a cider mill, a blacksmith shop, and a large farm. One mill was at the corner

Figure 5. *The Schultz Family Homestead in Schultzville, now the home of Craig and Mary Marshall. Photograph by Cynthia Koch.*

of Center and Clinton Corners–Schultzville Roads. The East Clinton Fire-house stands on the site of the old gristmill. Daniel H. was town supervisor in 1839–1840 and again in 1849.[12] He was married twice—first to Sally Ann (1811–1839), who died the year after Theodore was born. His second wife was Louisa Conger with whom he had a son who died young and two daughters, Susan A. and Ida M. [Tripp] (1852–1933). Four Schultz family graves were moved from Schultzville to Rhinebeck Cemetery on November 21, 1920. Daniel H. (1803–1858) and Louisa (1823–1904) are interred with Daniel's sons Theodore (1836–1862) and Daniel B. (1848–1858).[13]

The two surviving daughters' names are recorded in the *Journal of the Assembly of the State of New York* for 1862, when the assembly passed "An Act for the relief of Susan A. Schultz and Ida M. Schultz, infants, in certain lands devised to them by Daniel H. Schultz." A preamble described why an act of the legislature was necessary.

> Whereas Daniel H. Schultz, late of the town of Clinton, in the county of Dutchess, deceased, devised by his last will and testament to his daughters Susan A. Schultz and Ida M. Schultz, certain lands there-in described, and devised to his son, Theodore A. Schultz, in and by the same will, certain other lands designated as the homestead; and whereas the said Theodore A. Schultz, deceased, by his last will and testament, devised the said homestead to his two sisters, . . . and the said Susan A. and Ida M. are infants and desire to retain the said home-stead but cannotpay the legacies without the sale of the whole or some portion of the landsdevised them as aforesaid by the said David H. Schultz.[14]

The girls' mother turned to the legislature to delegate Reuben Rikert or another authorized "freeholder" to sell on their behalf the lands left to Ida and Susan by their father's will in order to satisfy the legacies of Theodore's will without having to sell the "homestead." Presumably those transactions were successful: the gifts that enabled the construction of the Christian Alliance Church and the Masonic Lodge were made without (we trust) the sale of the "homestead."

The homestead (Figure 5) still stands, proudly, in the heart of Schultzville as the home of Clinton Historical Society Vice President Craig Marshall and his wife Mary. How satisfying that the historical society was able to do the right thing and restore the Theodore Schultz portrait, giving us all a reason to reflect on our local history and the ties that bind us all in place over time.

[1]   James H. (James Hadden) Smith, *History of Duchess [Dutchess] County, New York* (Syracuse, NY: D. Mason and Co., 1882), p. 286 passim.

[2]   Ibid.

[3]   William P. McDermott, ed., *Clinton, Dutchess County, New York: A History of a Town* (Clinton Corners, NY: Town of Clinton Historical Society, 1987), p. 33.

[4]   Frank Hasbrouck, ed., *The History of Dutchess County, New York* (Poughkeepsie, NY: S.A. Matthieu, 1909), p. 440.

[5]   http://www.olivetreegenealogy.com/palatines/palatine-indentures.shtml   Accessed March 4, 2014.

[6]   Nancy V. Kelly, "Rhinebeck: Transition in 1799" in *The Hudson Valley Regional Review* Vol. 6, No. 2 (March 1989), p.94; McDermott, p. 62; Genealogical information on grave markers in Rhinebeck Reformed Dutch Cemetery.

[7]   Upton Lake Grange, "Town of Clinton: A Historical Review, 1959," for New York's Year of History 350th Hudson/Champlain Anniversary, p. 13

[8]   Quoted in McDermott, p. 49.

[9]   Hasbrouck, p. 276 reports that after 25 years of successful operations, it was discovered that the "grade of slate was too heavy for durable roofing purposes."

[10]   Ibid.

[11]   Kelly, p. 94.

[12]   Compiled from various sources including McDermott, p.62

[13]   Information from online record of burials, including photo of the grave marker, and indicates the relationship between Daniel, his two wives and sons as "calculated." http://www.findagrave.com/cgi-bin/fg.cgi?page=gr&GSln=Schultz&GSiman=1&GScid=2356654&GRid=92859248&

[14]   *Journal of the Assembly of the State of New York*, Friday, April 4, 1862, p. 687. The measure passed unanimously and was sent back to the Senate for ratification with minor amendments.

CENTENNIAL CELEBRATION

The Dutchess County Historical Society 1914–2014

by Eileen Mylod Hayden

Wild West showman and entrepreneur Col. William F. Cody eloquently expressed the following thought:

> As we look into the open fire for our fancies, so we are apt to study the dim past for the wonderful and sublime, forgetful that the present is a constant romance, and the happenings of today, which we count of little importance, are sure to startle somebody in the future, and engage the pen of the historian, philosopher and poet.[1]

Dutchess County historian Helen Wilkinson Reynolds, perhaps Cody's polar opposite, had a similar if more down-to-earth view. She wrote:

> In former times, the life of the people was little reckoned with by historians. History was seen as a study of the apex of the social pyramid and kings and kingdoms, campaigns and commanders filled the printed page…but they are effects, not causes. Causes lie deep at the base of the pyramid, imbedded in the life of all the people.[2]

These words from both sources embody the goal set by the founders announcing a need for "…an historical organization for the purpose of preserving for future reference events of importance to the people of the county."[3] Little did the fifty ladies and gentlemen who met in Pleasant Valley in April 1914 realize that they were launching an organization that would still be a vibrant, productive entity a century later, still committed to the founding goals.

These men and women were concerned that rapid technological growth, following a burgeoning industrial explosion of the late nineteenth/early twentieth century, would be a threat to the ideals, institutions, and relics of the past. Buildings of the colonial period were being demolished; furnishings were being tossed into disorganized attics as useless and outmoded. There was no organized system for preservation of the archives and artifacts of Dutchess County's past. The founders were also aware that, from the early to middle years of the nineteenth century, there had been a growing rift between rural and urban segments of the county. The growth of towns and cities threatened the rural way of life, economically, politically, and philosophically. Even art and architecture were very different. By the spring of 1914, when the first meeting of the Dutchess County Historical Society was held, it had been nearly fifty years since the end of the Civil War. Many of the founders were keenly aware of the importance of that event in the American past and of the documents connected to it. The men who had fought in that war would soon be gone—and, with them, their letters, photographs, and other materials associated with the war. Considering all these factors, the founders determined that a broad goal would be to collect, preserve and promote material relevant to the history of Dutchess County and the United States in a systematic way.

Although the organization was initially intended to be named the *Pleasant Valley Historical Society*, a motion by Doctor J.Wilson Poucher to substitute *Dutchess County Historical Society* prevailed.[4] Despite previous failed attempts to form a society devoted to local history, those present considered that this was the time to try again and so the proposed By-Laws were approved, with dues set at $1.00 per year.[5] The By-Laws of Dutchess County Historical Society (DCHS) have been amended and changed over the years, to reflect changing circumstances and technological advances, but the original purpose remains.

In a membership meeting in early 1915, Vassar College Professor James Baldwin spoke on the value of local archives and opened his address to the audience of thirty or so assembled at Vassar Institute with an observation that resonates to this day[6]:

> Americans are fonder of making history than preserving records or turning to the past for guidance and information. They are usually too busy to think of this.

Baldwin went on to issue a strong challenge:

> To keep the world's memory from fading by preserving the common places, the public records, the private records of religious institutions, families and businesses.

The speech sparked the listeners to take his advice and begin the task. By the close of 1915, there were 155 members, thirty-one of them women. In 1918, the State of New York granted a provisional charter and in 1983, a permanent charter. Baldwin remained closely associated with the society until his death in1950 and in his work as history professor and County Historian, he practiced what he had preached on that evening.[7]

Early members included first president, Henry Magill; John Sickley, first director of Poughkeepsie's library; Vincent Astor; Nelson House owner Horatio Bain; Miami Beach tycoon Harry Harkness Flagler; Hon. Edmund Platt; Hon. Franklin D. Roosevelt and his mother; Robert B. Suckley of *Wilderstein;* educator, literary critic and activist, Prof. Joel Spingarn; Poughkeepsie Mayor George Spratt; Alice Crary Sutcliff, a descendant of Madam Brett; banker, Oakleigh Thorne; haberdasher Frank Van Kleeck; and real estate broker Capt. Andrew Zabriskie (some early members shown in 1926 photo, Figure 1). Not all members were wealthy or luminaries, but all supported the aims of the society. A look at most of the membership lists as presented in the yearbooks would disclose a most interesting cross-section of county residents, with a smattering of New York City residents, all interested in local history.

Figure 1. *An outing to the Residence of Isaac S. Wheaton, Lithgow, New York, by the Dutchess County Historical Society, September 15, 1926. Detail (see complete photo on cover), from left standing: John J. Mylod, Frank V. Mylod, Helen Wilkinson Reynolds; seated from left: unknown, Dr. J. Wilson Poucher. Photograph (panoramic). Collection of the Dutchess County Historical Society.*

Many of the 1914 members made an imprint on their offspring, who followed the path blazed by the elders. George S. Van Vliet was followed on the board of trustees by his children Richard Van Vliet and later by his daughter Helena Van Vliet; Dr. Poucher by Franklyn Poucher. Frank Van Kleeck's son Baltus B. Van Kleeck became president of the society and Baltus B. Van Kleeck's son, Peter Van Kleeck, served as treasurer. Cousin Ralph Van Kleeck sat in the president's chair for a term. Robert B. Suckley, owner of *Wilderstein* influenced daughter Margaret "Daisy" Suckley, who became a trustee in 1950 and 1951. William Willis Reese, the society's president in 1937 was followed by Willis L. M. Reese as a trustee. At the death of John J. Mylod in 1936, his son, attorney Frank V. Mylod succeeded him as trustee. Mylod faithfully filled the chairs of president, secretary, trustee and Vice President for the City of Poughkeepsie for forty-one years, until 1977. He in turn was followed some years later by the first female president of the society, his daughter, this author.

I was succeeded as president by Mylod's son-in-law, John A. Wolf. Dynastic thoughts aside, it was the core beliefs in the value of local history that were imbued in a younger generation and provided continued stability to the society.

Figure 2. *Annual Meeting held in the open air at Rokeby, Red Hook, New York. 1992. John Wolf, standing, at left, was the President at that time. Photograph. Collection of Dutchess County Historical Society.*

Much of the society's first fifty years is captured in the meeting minutes of the Board of Trustees and the annual and semi-annual membership meetings. The minutes were printed in most editions of the yearbook until 1984. For the most part, the early trustees met at the Amrita Club or Adriance Memorial Library, with membership meetings held at the Nelson House, Vassar Institute, or Vassar College. As time passed, membership meetings were held in restaurants, churches and historic sites throughout the county. A member recalls an annual meeting held on the lawn of the National Parks Service offices at *Bellefield,* former home of original member the Hon. Thomas Newbold. It was a quintessential June day, with business meeting, buffet luncheon and a provocative guest speaker, Dr. William Emerson, Director of the Franklin D. Roosevelt Presidential Library.[8]

Members were elected by the executive committee of the board of trustees and presented for a vote at the annual meeting, perhaps giving rise to that notion that this was a socially or intellectually elite organization. Eventually, the presentation of names for membership was discontinued and payment of dues was the chief requirement to belong. There were three categories of membership: annual, life, and honorary. Initially, dues were $1.00 for an annual membership and *at least* $25.00 for a life member-

Figure 3. *Eileen Mylod Hayden, granddaughter and daughter of founders and early members of the Dutchess County Historical Society. Eileen became the first female President of the society (1984–1989) and later served as its Executive Director (1991–2007). She is shown here delivering a speech at an annual meeting in the early 1990s. Photograph. Collection of the Dutchess County Historical Society.*

ship. By 1950, dues had risen to $2.00. In 1964, the fiftieth anniversary of the society, life membership had risen to the $75 level. Members were duly recorded in most editions of the yearbook, although this practice was discontinued in 1984. Originally, deceased members and resignations were also published.

The Pilgrimage, the Silver Ribbon House Tour, the Road Rallye, and the Annual Awards Dinner

Again suggesting a certain level of member affluence for the early years of DCHS, the annual automobile tour of different sections of Dutchess County, officially referred to as "the pilgrimage" afforded members and their guests the opportunity to visit historic sites and homes with interpretation by owners or local historians. Over the intervening years, the annual trek visited all parts of the county, with the exception of the war years and the day following the death of President Kennedy. On several jaunts, busses transported the pilgrims as a measure to conserve gasoline or when parking was limited. The variety of sites and homes visited is extraordinary— Revolutionary War sites, *Troutbeck* in Amenia, *Rokeby* in Red Hook, radio broadcaster Lowell Thomas's home in Pawling, and Franklin Roosevelt's home (*Springwood*) in Hyde Park, to name a few. Pilgrims provided their own basket lunches and various church or grange groups tendered desserts and beverages. On a few occasions, the pilgrimage left the county to tour historic sites in Putnam, Orange, and Ulster counties.

Figure 4. *Road signs in eastern Dutchess, image from past Road Rallye. Photograph. Collection of Barbara Van Itallie.*

Figure 5. *Barbara Van Itallie, founder of Road Rallye. Recipient of Dutchess Award in 2011. Photograph. Collection of Barbara Van Itallie.*

Figure 6. *Dr. Sam Simon honored with the Dutchess Award at the Annual Awards Dinner, 2010. He was honored for his service to the community as an orthopedic surgeon and, after his retirement from medicine, as the founder of Hudson Valley Fresh, a co-operative for small dairy farm owners producing milk and milk products.*

Eventually, the pilgrimage ceased to be a popular jaunt for members and was discontinued. In 1992, it was reinvented as the Silver Ribbon Tour. Visits to various towns in the county involved the local historical societies and an army of docents trained to interpret the selected private and public sites of architectural and/or historic interest. Still later, the Road Rallye, a self-guided, fall driving tour—with listed historical sites of the area to be visited— was added to the society's programming (Figures 4 and 5). The scenic delights of the county combined with a clever quiz and stops along the way made this a popular outing.

Beginning in 1999, the society instituted an annual fund-raising dinner in the fall at which we honored individuals who had contributed to the promotion of history in Dutchess County (Figure 6). We gave a prize named the "Dutchess Award" for service in the community. Over time, we added two more awards: the Helen Wilkinson Reynolds Award for scholarship in writing about the history of the county, and the Business of Historical Distinction Award for a business of long standing that contributed to the county. This lively event continues to be an effective way of honoring individuals and bringing people together.

Helen Wilkinson Reynolds

No history of the society would be complete without mention of Helen Wilkinson Reynolds (Figure 7). Very early in the life of the society, Reynolds embraced its work. Without an academic degree or even a high school diploma, she made an indelible mark on the society until her death in 1943 and even to this day. Reynolds served on a variety of society's committees and was appointed the yearbook editor in 1921. It was her contention that the primary work of the society should be the publication of well-researched histories and articles. It was as editor that she flourished, as did the society.

Her friendships, collaborations, social and professional contacts gave her entrée to private resource material. Many of the yearbook articles bear her name and just as many are unsigned but bear the stamp of her sound research. The 1940 Year Book contained fourteen articles; six by Dr. J. Wilson Poucher, six by Reynolds, and two by unidentified authors (in all probability, the work of Reynolds).[9]

Figure 7. *Helen Wilkinson Reynolds (1875–1943), "a remarkable woman who had a profound effect on the ... history of the Society" for her contributions in research, scholarship, and publication. She was the editor of the society's Yearbook for many years, authoring over sixty essays on a variety of topics. Photograph from* Dutchess County Historical Society Yearbook, *Volume 78, 1993, p. 4.*

Her successful research partnerships with Dr. Poucher, W. Willis Reese, and Franklin D. Roosevelt added to the luster of the society. With FDR, she shared a unique and enduring friendship, cemented by their mutual interest in local history. Indeed, FDR intended for her a key role in his presidential library. Roosevelt had served as the society's Town of Hyde Park Vice-President, representing Hyde Park until his death in 1945, and as Hyde Park Town Historian from 1926–1932. As such, he had produced research on Dutch colonial architecture which led directly to Reynolds 1929 publication of *Dutch Houses in the Hudson Valley Before 1776*.[10] He continued to collaborate with her until her death. Their correspondence reveals delight in delving into and solving historical puzzles. As President of the United States, Roosevelt had access to global resources and the British Admiralty was one such contact. From the Admiralty, he requested the records of British naval activity on the Hudson River during the American Revolution. The response became two yearbook articles, published in 1935 and 1936.[11]

Dr. Poucher was another of her chief collaborators and together they gathered 19,000 inscriptions of gravestones that became the classic *Old Gravestones of Dutchess County, New York,* published in 1924. Poucher was eminent in his own right, publishing a similar work on the gravestones of Ulster County.[12] He also published a volume on wildflowers, and, in 1930, a memoir of his life as a physician, with an introduction by Reynolds.[13]

Reynolds collaborated with W. Willis Reese on *Eighteenth Century Records of the Portion of Dutchess County, New York, that was included in Rombout Precinct and the original Town of Fishkill;*[14] and with Edith A. Roberts on *The Role of Plant Life in the History of Dutchess County.*[15] This latter, 1938 work contained an insert of an early aerial view of the county, innovative for the time. She was allied with John J. Mylod in the cause of preservation of long neglected county records. Mylod, as City of Poughkeepsie Historian, used his prestige to lobby for her appointment as County Historian in 1927. Numerous others, including Vassar College President Henry Noble MacCracken, Vassar History professor Lucy Maynard Salmon, and photographer Margaret DeMott Brown were her colleagues. Prof. Salmon's view that critical thinking was the backbone of sound research had an influence on Reynolds and her careful research methods. Her editorial skills and research ethic were passed on to Amy Pearce Ver Nooy, who succeeded her as yearbook editor.

After the death of Helen Wilkinson Reynolds, the New York State Historian eulogized her as:

> ...for so many years the editor of the excellent Dutchess County Historical Society yearbook and other beautiful works on Dutchess County history.... May her name never be forgotten in the county of her delight.[16]

The Yearbook

The inaugural issue of the yearbook is dated 1914–1915 and covered the activities of the birth of the society. The slim, gray volume contained a copy of the Hudson Valley portion of the Joseph Sauthier map printed in London in 1779, photographs of Pleasant Valley Library where the society's organization meeting was held, the First Reformed Dutch Church, Fishkill, a plaque listing early clergymen of that church, and Brick House Farm. Also included were committee reports, reprints of news accounts of the early meetings, the first By Laws, and the society's first try at fund raising, a conveniently simple description of the wording for bequests to the new organization. The volume closed with listings of the members.[17]

Subsequent editions have contained interesting and insightful work by local historians producing a wealth of information on the history of Dutchess

County—a rich mix of research, reminiscence, recollection. Some of the articles were written by renowned authors and historians such as cultural critic Lewis Mumford and, of course, Helen Reynolds, who contributed sixty-three articles in total. The current index of articles is a wonderful source of the breadth and depth of subjects covered. The maps alone, contained in multiple editions, would make a book. Many editions are illustrated by drawings, paintings, and the wonderful photography of Margaret De Mott Brown, among others. Color photography first appeared in Volume 80 to illustrate the paintings of Jerome Deyo. To help defray the growing cost of publication, advertising first appeared in 1985. Several issues followed themes such as art in Dutchess County, county women of note, county poets and their work, and essays in honor of Poughkeepsie's 300th anniversary. For many years, both Helen Reynolds and Amy Ver Nooy used leftover space at the close of an article to include "squibs" from old newspapers that struck them as interesting. One such item read:

> Jenny Lind was offered some thirty thousand pounds to sing at the Imperial Concerts at the Court of Russia. Jenny's significant negative to the offer was "Hungary." Great is the triumph of genius, when the nightingale is too much for the bear.
>
> *The Journal & Poughkeepsie Eagle*, May 11, 1850[18]

The Collection

The stated objective for the society as set forth in the original By-Laws was to discover, procure and preserve whatever may relate to the natural, civil, literary and ecclesiastical history of the State of New York and particularly

Figure 8. *The Glebe House, 635 Main Street, Poughkeepsie, New York. Built 1767 for the Reverend John Beardsley, priest of Christ Church, and his family. The Rev. Beardsley, ever loyal to King and Country [England], fled to the relative safety of New York City in 1777. His wife, children, black female servant, and her children followed. The house was originally built as a Dutch-style home with two front doors, then remodeled to a more "modern," gracious English-style home by the DeReimer family who took ownership in 1796. Photograph. Collection of the Dutchess County Historical Society.*

Figure 9. *The Dutch Kas (tall cupboard), American, late seventeenth- to early eighteenth-century, displaying American textiles and other items. At the Glebe House, Main Street, Poughkeepsie, New York. Photograph by Charlotte Jenks Lewis Photography (charlottejenkslewis.com). Collection of the Dutchess County Historical Society.*

of the County of Dutchess.[19] The scope of the collection has narrowed over time. Today it relates primarily to the history of Dutchess County and contiguous sections of counties once part of Dutchess, from the time of the arrival of the earliest Native Americans until the present day.

A significant portion of the collection is kept at the Glebe House, where it is displayed as part of the historic house museum exhibit (Figures 8 & 9). Since 1930, when the Glebe House was renovated by the society and the Junior League, and converted into a small historic museum, the society has been adding to the collections for the interpretation of the period when the house was built—1767—and the following decades.

The part of the collection housed at Clinton House contains family bibles, diaries, paintings, wills, maps, paper ephemera, newspapers, furniture and furnishings, photographs, Dutchess County post cards, cemetery records, and more. The collections provide the basis for research, exhibition, education, and publications (Figure 10).

More important than the volume or variety of items, collection management and care is guided by a policy created to seek, collect, and preserve these items, which are held in trust for the people of Dutchess County. The collection is the core of the Dutchess County Historical Society. Most of the activities the public sees—lectures, workshops, symposia, exhibits, and publications—stem from the collection and so its proper and systematic care is vital. Trustees provide overall governance, and staff administer the collection policy. Fund-raising provides for its professional care. A Capital Campaign begun in 1982 raised over $160,000. A current campaign seeks $1,000,000 for the endowment. The administration of the endowment fund is managed by the Community Foundations of the Hudson Valley.

Members and the broader community are the true beneficiaries of these preservation efforts.

Figure 10. *From left: Melodye Moore, Trustee and Head of Collections at the Dutchess County Historical Society, with Michele Phillips, paper conservator, Bureau of Historic Sites, Peebles Island, New York State Office of Parks, Recreation and Historic Preservation, Cohoes, New York, examining a poster from the Hubbard Collection, a large new collection from a family that owned an apple orchard from 1839 through the 1960s. December 2012. Photograph by Candace Lewis.*

Glebe House and Clinton House

Built in 1767 as a residence for the rector of Christ Church, the Glebe House housed a variety of owners after Rev. John Beardsley and his family were exiled from Poughkeepsie in 1777 because of his Loyalist beliefs. Once encompassing nearly 250 acres, the grounds had dwindled by 1929. It was then that the sturdy brick house, one of the oldest documented homes in Poughkeepsie, was saved from demolition by the combined efforts of Dutchess County Historical Society and the Junior League of Poughkeepsie. Their fund raising effort (including a raffle for a Whippet automobile[20]), combined with the city's contribution of half the purchase price, was successful and the house was purchased from florist Conrad Gindra.[21] In record time, the mortgage was paid and the house was then donated to the City of Poughkeepsie to be jointly operated by the society and the Junior League as a house museum. Landscaping was to be the contribution of the Poughkeepsie Garden Club. Over the intervening years, countless children and adults have taken interpreted tours (Figure 11) that explained life as it was lived in the eighteenth and early nineteenth centuries.

Almost every trustee meeting contained a Glebe House report. Meeting minutes reveal the difficulties of keeping the venerable house in good repair, furnishing it appropriately, researching the history of its inhabitants, and hiring caretakers and managers. A contract with the City, spelling out responsibilities of each entity, has been in place since 1929. The commitment to Glebe House remains a vital role for DCHS. Both the League and DCHS have done yeoman's service on behalf of the Glebe House.

Clinton House, so-named by the Daughters of the American Revolution (DAR) to honor George Clinton—the first Governor of New York State (1777–1796 and 1801–1804), and the Vice-President of the United States (1805–1812), under both Thomas Jefferson and James Madison. The house was originally built about 1765 for Hugh Van Kleeck and his wife.[22] In 1780 the stone house became the home of Udney Hay, late of the Continental Army Quartermaster Corps. Following a serious fire, the house was rebuilt by artisans from Washington's headquarters. While the repairs took place, Hay resided in the empty Glebe House.

Figure 11. *Katherine Feeks, Trustee and docent, introducing elementary school children to the Glebe House and life in Poughkeepsie around the time of the American Revolutionary War (1776-1781). Early 1990s. Photograph. Collection of the Dutchess County Historical Society.*

Clinton House was the center of much activity during New York's Convention to ratify the U.S. Constitution, which was held in Poughkeepsie. There were many delegates from all over the state staying in Poughkeepsie, and after-hour meetings to discuss the proposed Constitution of the United States were held at Clinton House because of its good size. But by the end of the nineteenth century, the house was in poor shape. The DAR, looking for a meeting space for its new chapter, discovered the now empty Clinton House, purchased the house, and in 1900 turned it over to Gov. Theodore Roosevelt for the people of the State of New York. The DAR still maintains a room with its collection and holds an annual meeting in Clinton House.

Home for the Dutchess County Historical Society

For sixty-five years, DCHS was a peripatetic institution, with its meetings, papers and collections held in various locations. The third floor of Adriance Memorial Library, now a part of the Poughkeepsie Public Library District, was the major site for the collection. Space at Vassar Institute and the FDR Library was utilized as well. In addition, the Glebe House held the furnishings and objects relevant to that house. As the collections grew, reference to a more permanent space began to occur in the minutes of the trustee meetings. In 1976, member Jesse Effron suggested the creation of a museum-research center.[23] Taking up this thought, the board appointed trustee Kenneth Toole to study the possibilities of Effron's idea and submit a report. Toole's committee met with representatives of Vassar Institute, Marist College, and Franklin D. Roosevelt Library. Toole's final report offered choices: Accept the FDR Library's offer of talent and space or Vassar Institute space as a museum.[24] The board agreed with Toole that DCHS was not yet ready to function as a museum and wished more time to assess his report. Adriance Library, running out of space for its own collection, requested removal of the DCHS non-book collection. Discussion continued on how to achieve creation of a museum and/or research center. In 1979, Effron, and newcomers to the discussion—Franklin Roosevelt Jr. and Hamilton Fish Jr.—met with DCHS President Dr. Franklin Butts and his committee.[25] Both Fish and Roosevelt were confident that a dynamic program for a DCHS-run history center would bring in funding. But the trustees urged caution in proceeding with this idea. At this juncture, New York State's Clinton House became a possibility. The board decided to pursue this opportunity and the State was receptive to the DCHS committee's inquiry.[26]

Minutes of the May 1979 trustees meeting reveal that serious discussions regarding the lease of Clinton House had taken place with the State of New York. At the May meeting, the trustees spent ample time in the building and in considering all opinions, including questions regarding the permanence the new space being offered. Afterward, the following motion was offered:

> That the Society do enter into an Agreement with the State of New York for the use of the Clinton House by the Dutchess County Historical Society as a Research and Educational Center; and that said Agreement be approved subject to such changes suggested by the Society, Counsel, and the Direction Committee; and that the parties be permitted to sign the agreement provided the aforementioned provisions have been negotiated.[27]

The motion was passed, with one abstention[28] For thirty-five years the agreement has been renewed and has remained in place.

The move to Clinton House was a pivotal point in the history of DCHS. It was a fine opportunity to consolidate the safe storage of the collection under one roof, with museum practices supervised by professional staff. The State made structural changes to adapt the building for its new use, and the move was completed by 1980. A capital campaign raised funds to further complete interior changes to Clinton House, with a Research Library dedicated to former president Dr. Franklin Butts for his foresight in the successful completion of the partnership with the State of New York. Funds also were applied to hiring professional staff. The first Executive Director at Clinton House was former trustee, Melodye Moore, whose training in the museum field made her an ideal choice. Her leadership paved the way for a broader community role for DCHS.

Figure 12. *The Honorable Sandra Day O'Connor, Justice of the Supreme Court of the United States speaking on the occasion of the seventy-fifth anniversary of the Dutchess County Historical Society. Bardavon Opera House, Market Street, Poughkeepsie, NY. 1989. Photograph. Collection of the Dutchess County Historical Society.*

With the new space and hiring of staff, the board had to adjust to its new role as policy makers and not the "hands on" managers of DCHS. This was difficult at first, but all concerned adjusted.

Grants from public and private sources have supplemented the funds that had been established over the years. Funds had been used mainly for publication of the yearbook, newsletters, Glebe House maintenance, office supplies, pilgrimages and meetings. The move to Clinton House increased the need for funds. The funds named for Helen Reynolds, William Platt Adams and Carolyn Wells, along with membership dues and bequests, had been the main sources of income for DCHS.[29] The New York State Council on the Arts, Institute of Museum Services, Community Development Block Grants, the McCann Foundation, the Dyson Foundation, among others, have provided for collection care and management, educational programming, development of Black History materials, and after school programs for at-risk students.

A unique opportunity for the society initiated by the DCHS Black History committee, an archeological project in Hyde Park, was begun in 2001 with initial funding from the Charlotte Cunneen Hackett Trust,[30] followed by grants from the Dyson Foundation. Under the auspices of DCHS and with the agreement of the Town of Hyde Park, the historical significance of an eighteenth-mid nineteenth century enclave of freed blacks and former slaves within the Village of Hyde Park is still being explored.

The society celebrated its fiftieth anniversary in 1964 with a meeting and dinner held at the Presbyterian Church in Pleasant Valley, the town of its birth. Amendments to the By Laws were passed, three of the society's charter members were cited as still participating members and former president Frank Mylod spoke of the society's history. He ended with movies of several of the earlier pilgrimages.[31]

The seventy-fifth anniversary was a year- long celebration of events, culminating with an evening program at the Bardavon. Toasts and citations for the society were followed by Supreme Court Justice Sandra Day O'Connor (Figure 12), who spoke on the passage of the Judiciary Act of 1789.[32]

The Centennial Celebration

The society has much to celebrate in its centennial year. The accomplishments and contributions of a century by society officers, trustees, staff, and volunteers are manifold. They are highlighted by a body of significant publications in addition to the Year Book; by work to accomplish preservation of the earliest county records; by the effort of many years to document and preserve the county milestones; by establishing a presence at Clinton House as a local history educational center; by collaborating with local government for the celebration of significant anniversaries in the nation, state, and county; by preserving the eighteenth century Glebe House and using it as an educational tool; by publicly advocating preservation of our county's historic treasures; by lobbying for appointment of a county historian; by sponsorship of informative lectures, trips, and conferences for the dissemination of Dutchess County history.

Crossing the threshold of the society's next century is challenging but exciting. The vision and flexibility to seize opportunities for further growth and development as a vibrant organization will launch Dutchess County on its next hundred years. A new generation must take up the challenge.

1   *Year Book of the Dutchess County Historical Society*, Vol. 1, 1914–1915, p.5.

2   Helen W. Reynolds, *Dutch Houses in the* Hudson *Valley before 1776* (Reprinted, New York: Dover Books, 1965), pp. 3–4.

3   *Year Book of the Dutchess County Historical Society,* Vol. 1, 1914–1915, p. 5.

4   *Year Book of the Dutchess County Historical Society*, Vol. 1, 1914–1915, p. 6.

5   Ibid. The minutes refer to an earlier attempt to form a society. In 1844, the New York State Legislature passed a bill on behalf of the People of New York incorporating a Dutchess County Historical Society, according to the *Laws of the State of New York*, 1844, p. 230, Chapter 202. "Act to incorporate Dutchess County Historical Society passed by two-thirds vote of the New York State Senate and Assembly, representing the people of New York." That society failed to endure.

6   *Year Book of the Dutchess County Historical Year Book* Vol. 1, 1914-1915. Also published in James F. Baldwin, Ph.D., "Value of Local Archives," address reported in *Poughkeepsie News Press* January 16,1915.

7   *Year Book of the Dutchess County Historical Society*, Vol. 35, 1950, p. 20.

8   Personal communication from DCHS member Benjamin S. Hayden, III.

9   "Table of Contents," *Year Book of the Dutchess County Historical Society*, Vol.25, 1940, p. 6.

10 Introduction, Roosevelt Professional Award, Local Government Historians, New York State Museum Available at https://www.nysm.nysed.gov/services/historian/srvfdr.html

11 F.D. Roosevelt, "Events on Hudson's River," *Year Book of the Dutchess County Historical Society*, Vol. 20, 1935, and "The Congress and the Montgomery" Vol. 21, 1936.

12 J. Wilson Poucher, *Old Gravestones of Ulster County, New York* (Ulster County Historical Society, 1931).

13 J. Wilson Poucher, *Reminiscences Personal and Professional1859-1939*, introduction by Helen W. Reynolds (Poughkeepsie, NY: Lindmarks Books, 1930).

14 *Eighteenth Century Records of the Portion of Dutchess County, New York, that was included in Rombout Precinct and the Town of Fishkill,* Collected by William Willis Reese, Edited by Helen W. Reynolds, Collections of the Dutchess County Historical Society, Vol.VI, 1938.

15 Edith A. Roberts and Helen W. Reynolds, *The Role of Plant Life in the History of Dutchess County* (Poughkeepsie, New York: Lansing Broas Printing Company, 1938).

16 *Year Book of the Dutchess County Historical Society*, Vol. 28, 1943, p.19.

17 Year Book of the Dutchess County Historical Society, Vol. 1, 1914–1915.

18 *Year Book of the Dutchess County Historical Society*, Vol.49, 1964, p.38.

19 *Year Book of the, Dutchess County Historical Society,* Vol.1, 1914–1915, p.25.

20 Raffle ticket found in author's personal ephemera.

21 *The Glebe House, Poughkeepsie, New York, 1767,* Dutchess County Historical Society, May 1967.

[22] Edmund Platt, *The Eagle's History of Poughkeepsie, New York, 1683–1905* (Poughkeepsie, NY: Dutchess County Historical Society, 1987; facsimile of the original 1905 edition), p.32.

[23] Meeting minutes, September 1976, *Year Book of the Dutchess County Historical Society*, Vol. 61–62, p. 9.

[24] Meeting minutes, May 1977, Year Book of the Dutchess County Historical Society, Vol. 61–62, p.13.

[25] Meeting minutes, February 1979, *Year Book of the Dutchess County Historical Society*, Vol. 64, p.11.

[26] Meeting minutes, May 1979, *Year Book of the Dutchess County Historical Society*, Vol. 64, p. 15.

[27] Meeting minutes, May 1979, Year Book of the Dutchess County Historical Society, Vol. 64, p. 15.

[28] There was no attendance record and no mention of who abstained.

[29] The Reynolds Fund was a memorial fund created by the trustees at Helen Reynolds's death. The W. Platt Adams Fund was created by his bequest. Carolyn Wells of Rhinebeck, New York, died in 1938 but her estate was not settled until 1969, at which time DCHS, along with Northern Dutchess Hospital, received the benefit.

[30] Charlotte Cunneen Hackett lived at Hackett Hill, in Hyde Park, which is now town parkland. The DCHS archeology project is conducted on part of this property.

[31] Meeting minutes, Year Book of Dutchess County Historical Society, Vol.49, 1964, p.13.

[32] The 75th Anniversary committee, chaired by John E. Mack, was aided in its search for a suitable speaker by the Hon. Albert M. Rosenblatt. At the committee's request, DCHS chartered a plane to fly Justice Sandra Day O'Connor to Poughkeepsie from Washington, D.C. Further, the President (this author) was sent to welcome her and make any decisions regarding cancellation due to weather. It was a fine opportunity for me to describe the society and the rich history of the Hudson Valley region as we flew above it.

The Dutchess County Society in The City of New York

by Melodye Moore

From 1861 to 1865, Americans fought Americans during a civil war that nearly tore the country apart. The joint sense of solidarity that was a hallmark of the Revolution was washed away on the bloody battlefields of places like Bull Run, Gettysburg, and Vicksburg. Lincoln's April 14, 1865 assassination cast a further pall over an already exhausted and demoralized America. Yet one year later, John L. Campbell, a professor at Wabash College in Crawfordsville, Indiana, offered an optimistic suggestion to the mayor of Philadelphia – why not celebrate the 100th Anniversary of the signing of the Declaration of Independence with an exposition. Over the next six years, Campbell continued to enlist support for his idea and, on March 3, 1872, the United States Centennial Committee was formed. Four more years of planning culminated with the May 10, 1876, opening of the international exposition that was set on 285 acres, hosted thirty-seven nations, and showcased numerous industrial exhibits. The years of preparation for America's first international exhibition sparked a renewed patriotic fervor that attracted a reported ten million visitors, twenty percent of the national population. The exposition helped to recast the country from a land torn apart by war into a new industrial power that could accomplish anything.

The wave of patriotism that followed the November 10 closing of the exposition continued, and Americans became intensely interested in the beginnings of the country. This interest trickled down to the state and local level. In 1882, James H. Smith published his *History of Dutchess County, New York, 1683–1882*. Smith's comprehensive historical overview of the county and each of the towns in the county was undoubtedly timed to coincide with the upcoming 200th anniversary of the founding of the county which would take place on November 11, 1883. Two years later in 1885 the Holland Society was incorporated by the State of New York, and "The History of the Holland Society" attributes the origins of the Society to the fact that the nation was "experiencing a vast migration of peoples from eastern and southern Europe to work its farms, factories, and mines," and this wave of newcomers, along with the surging Industrial Revolution led to many looking "to the past in order to maintain a footing in a rapidly changing present."[1] Nationally this period of patriotism and nostalgia resulted in the formation of the Sons of the American Revolution on April 4, 1889, the 100th anniversary of the inauguration of George Washington as the nation's first President. The following year, on October 11, the Daughters of the American Revolution were formed.

The Birth of the Dutchess County Society in The City of New York

Amidst all this enthusiasm for things past, the Dutchess County Society was born.[2] In December of 1896, seven men met at the West 81st Street home of Dr. Charles G. Kerley to discuss the forming of a society in the City of New York that would be composed of former residents of Dutchess County. Present in addition to Dr. Kerley were: William S. Cross, A.P. Cross, Walter R. Quick, J. Walter Righter, Dr. Irving Townsend, and the Honorable Alfred T. Ackert. The group reassembled on January 30, 1897 at which time it was reported that a certificate of incorporation had been filed on January 13. The purposes for which the organization was formed were stated to be: "benevolent, charitable, literary and historical purposes, to perpetuate existing friendships among its members and to keep alive memories of Dutchess County."[3] The member must also be "a man of good social standing."[4] The men moved quickly to interest others in joining and the first regular meeting of the society was held on February 9, 1897, at the East 55th Street home of Dr. Townsend. Dr, Kerley was elected the first President. A little over a month later, on March 26, 1897, the society held the first of many banquets to celebrate Dutchess County and their own personal connections to their ancestral homes. Held at the Murray Hill Hotel, the first banquet was attended by thirty-nine members and guests.[5] The society was off to a rousing start.

Figure 1. *Diagram of the official insignia of the society. The insignia depicted the plow and the sheaf of wheat that is still part of the official Dutchess County seal. The insignia also incorporated two lions rampant supporting the shield which is surmounted by a crown, presumably that of the Duchess of York, namesake for the county. Members were required to wear the insignia, suspended from a ribbon, at all functions.*

The formation of the Dutchess County Society was not only the outgrowth of renewed patriotism, it was also part of a surge in the creation of clubs representing geographical sections of the county. According to a February 16, 1902, article published in *The New York Times*, "The State and county clubs in New York have within the past few months been increasing so rapidly that it is hard to keep track of them."[6] At the time, there were societies representing many states and groups of states, and at least a dozen New York counties—Dutchess being one—had their own county societies. Apparently not everyone found these societies to be beneficial. The same *New York Times* article recounts that "when the late Gen. W.T. Sherman was invited on one occasion to make a speech to the Ohio Society of New York city, he declined with these words:

> No, I will not speak at your dinner, I have always refused to join such organizations because I believe they cherish sectionalism, and I'm not going to begin making speeches for them now.[7]

Most people did not share Sherman's opinion and many men were reported to belong to four or five different clubs at once. The New York City social calendar was so full of club dinners and entertainment that hardly a winter week passed without the opportunity to attend some regional club activity.

A proposal to form a federation of county societies was apparently considered during 1901, but at a meeting of the Dutchess County Society, held on December 4 of that year and reported on in *The New York Times*, about one hundred members of a membership of 105 did not endorse the idea.[8] The following year however, two months after the publication of the aforementioned article, the clubs came together to jointly sponsor a dinner on the anniversary of De Witt Clinton's birthday.[9] Twenty years later, the Hudson Valley clubs had obviously forged a much closer relationship and jointly published the first volume of *The Home County Magazine*. The magazine, which was to come out monthly, was intended to "promote the interests of the County Societies of Albany, Dutchess, Greene, Ulster, Orange, Columbia, Rennsealaer, and the Daughters of The Columbia County Historical Society, Inc. in New York City."[10] The publisher of the magazine was Joseph Drake of 116 Nassau Street in the city and the price for the magazine was twenty-five cents per copy. A yearly subscription cost $2.50. The magazine included articles of local history, a page dedicated to the activities of each society and advertisements for local companies such as Luckey, Platt and Company. The August 1923 edition included a reference to a July 1, 1922, volume that reported that a committee would be formed in the fall to discuss the establishment of a permanent headquarters for the combined societies. It is not known if that was ever accomplished since only one edition of the magazine has been located.

The Founding Members

Since the original purpose of the organization was to "keep alive memories of Dutchess County"[11] in the minds of men who had left the county to become residents of New York City, it is not surprising that the first leaders of the Society seemed more at home in the big city than back on the farms or in the villages of their ancestral homeland. Most of these men, and it is important to note that this was a "men only" club, were well respected professionals who had carved out successful careers for themselves in the city.

Dr. Charles Gilmore Kerley convened the meeting to discuss the formation of the Society and was subsequently elected the first president. Kerley was one of seven children born to James and Eliza Kerley of Red Hook, New York. The family farm, located on the corner of the Post Road and West Kerley's Corners Road, included 388 acres. Dr. Kerley's father worked locally as a contractor and a United States Revenue Collector. Kerley left Red Hook to become a physician and was reputed to be the "most well known child physician in the United States."[12] He was a critic of prepared food for infants and a noted lecturer and author. His love for Dutchess County apparently did not influence him in his choice of weekend homes since he established his rural retreat, "Hilltop," in Sharon, Connecticut. At his death on September 7, 1945, his estate was valued at $1,638,292[13].

Charles's brother, Abram Pitcher Kerley, was the A.P. Kerley present at the organizing meetings. Five years older than Charles, he too moved away from Red Hook and became a New York City chemist and pharmacist.[14]

Alfred T. Ackert was born on April 15, 1840 in Rhinebeck, the son of Jacob H. and Lydia Maria Moore Ackert. He was educated at the Amenia Seminary and Fort Edward Institute, in Washington County, and graduated from Albany Law School in 1863. In the fall of that same year, he joined the New York City law firm of Wetmore and Bowne.[15] Described by his detractors as "a young, third-rate, but energetic, pushing lawyer and politician," [16] he was elected as a Democrat from the 2nd District of Dutchess County to serve in the 91st New York State Legislative session that ran from January 7 through May 6, 1868. He was not re-nominated the following year. Having been elected to office from Dutchess County, he must have maintained a primary residence in Rhinebeck and, in 1869, he became the President of the Rhinebeck Printing and Publishing Company. In 1873 he was nominated by New York City Mayor William F. Havemeyer to the position of Police Justice. Caught up in the bitter New York City politics of the time, his nomination was rejected by the New York City Board of Aldermen. Undeterred he remained politically active and, in April of 1875, he was appointed by then Governor Tilden as Justice of the 7th District Civil Court for the unexpired term of recently deceased John A. Stemmer. At the time *The New York Times* reported that Ackert "has been since the Tweed regime expired an ardent supporter and warm personal friend of John Kelly and Governor Tilden."[17] Ackert was the Secretary of the Tammany General committee and Scribe of the General Council of Tammany Sachems. The principal speaker at the second annual banquet of the Dutchess County Society held on February 28, 1898, at the Waldorf-Astoria, Ackert titled his speech "Dutchess County In Colonial Times." The speech was later published. Ackert died on April 14, 1901 and is buried in the Wurtemburg Cemetery in Rhinebeck.

William Spencer Cross, born in 1866, was the son of Dr. William and Anna Marie Cross of Rhinebeck. Their family home at 6435 Montgomery Street, built circa 1845, is now part of the Delamater Inn complex. William worked as a reporter for the *Rhinebeck Gazette* before moving to New York City sometime between 1890 and 1894. There he assumed a position with the magazine *The Iron Age* and became deeply involved with the Republican politics of the city. In 1908, he was a delegate to the state GOP convention and served as clerk of the Municipal Court, Ninth District for many years. He died on July 13, 1940, and was survived by his wife Jessie and daughter Dorothy.

J. Walter Righter was born in 1861 in Pine Plains. It is not known when he relocated to New York City, but in 1887, he opened a decorating firm and served as the senior member and President of Righter and Kolb, an interior design firm located on Madison Avenue. A life-long bachelor, he died on July 30, 1927. His obituary noted that he was "active in Dutchess County organizations," and was "a member of several New York clubs, including the Art in Trades Club, the Transportation Club and the National Republican Club, where he was a member of the House Committee."[18] In addition to being a founding member of the Dutchess County Society, he served as Chair of the Banquet Committee in 1908 and as a Director from 1912–1918—according to the incomplete records of the Society.

There is less biographical information available about the remaining two founding members. Irving Townsend was, like Charles G. Kerley, a physician. He was an active member of the Homeopathic Society of New York

City and was the author of "Condition of The Respiratory Passages Resulting From Automobiling," which was presented at the 51st Annual Meeting of the Homeopathic Society in 1902.[19] Townsend stayed active in the Society for at least twenty years serving as President from 1903–1905, and then with Righter as a Director in 1908 and from 1912–1918. He was also a member of various banquet and speaker committees. Walter Remington Quick was born on January 14, 1867, in the Town of Rhinebeck. The 1870 census lists his location as Rhinecliff, but his presence at the first meeting suggests he had relocated to Manhattan prior to 1896. He is listed as a member of the Banquet and Membership Committees in the program booklet for the Eighteenth Annual Banquet in 1914. He died on January 9, 1925, and is buried in Rhinebeck.

The Membership

A blank "Application for Membership" in the Haight Family Collection sets out the eligibility requirements for membership in the Society (Figures 2 & 3). The applicant had to document that he had been born in Dutchess County and give his birthplace, or demonstrate that he was the son of someone born in Dutchess County, or was presently or formerly a resident of Dutchess County for at least two years. The application had to be signed by a proposer and a seconder and submitted for review. The annual dues payment was $3.00 and had to be sent to the Treasurer. The form was printed after 1910. A life membership cost was $50.00.

Growth in the ranks of those joining the club must have been dramatic. By January 1, 1910, the membership had grown from the thirty-nine members and guests who were present at the first banquet in 1897 to 440 mem-

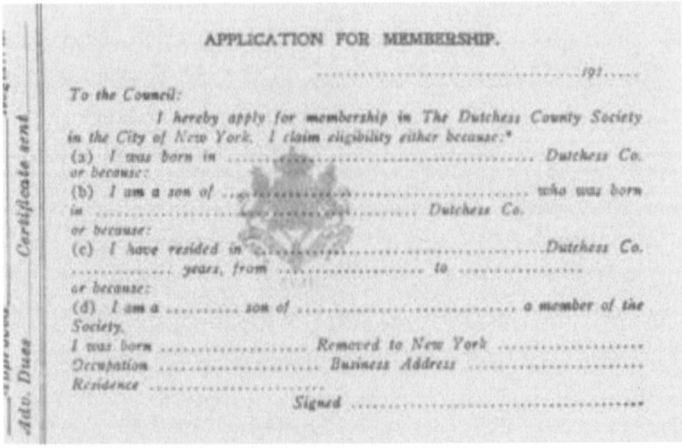
APPLICATION FOR MEMBERSHIP.

....191.....

To the Council:

I hereby apply for membership in The Dutchess County Society in the City of New York. I claim eligibility either because:*

(a) I was born in .... Dutchess Co.
or because:
(b) I am a son of .... who was born in .... Dutchess Co.
or because:
(c) I have resided in .... Dutchess Co.
.... years, from .... to ....
or because:
(d) I am a .... son of .... a member of the Society.

I was born .... Removed to New York ....
Occupation .... Business Address ....
Residence ....

Signed ....

Certificate sent ____ Adv. Dues ____

Figure 2. *Application for Membership in the Society. First section, detail. Post dates 1910. Haight Family Collection.*

Figure 3. *Application for Membership in the Society. Map of Dutchess County, third page, detail. Post dates 1910. Haight Family Collection.*

bers. By January 1, 1912, there were 525 members and, a year later, on February 1, 1913, 554 men had joined. At the end of 1913, there were 590 members and, by the middle of 1914, the Society had enrolled 600 men.[20]

It appears that, during the early years of the Society, the membership and the leadership came from men whose primary residence was New York City. By 1903, however, men with names more recognizable in Dutchess County history—such as Levi P. Morton, Henry Belden Ketcham and John Jacob Astor—were being elected as officers. This trend seems to have continued and, by 1910, many prominent members and leaders had no residence in the city and participated in the organization from their residences in Dutchess County. Among the names listed as Regents in 1910 who had no reported homes in New York City were Peter H. Troy of Poughkeepsie, the Hon. Robert W. Chanler of Red Hook, Col. Archibald Rogers of Hyde Park, and Capt. Andrew C. Zabriskie of Barrytown. The general membership included prominent Poughkeepsians Peter Adriance, Charles Arnold, Horatio Bain, Ralph and Allison Butts, George Collingwood, and John E. Mack.

It wasn't until 1914, with the establishment of the Dutchess County Historical Society, that a local organization existed whose mission was to preserve the history of Dutchess County. Unlike the Dutchess County Society, the historical society was, from its first meeting, welcoming of women and was more interested in preserving the county's ancient documents and promoting scholarship about the history of the county than "celebrating" the county's history. An examination of the founding officers of the Dutchess County Historical Society reveals that only Dr. Irving Le Roy of Pleasant Valley was a member of the Dutchess County Society in 1910. Things hadn't changed much by 1917 when only two of the nineteen members of the leadership of the Dutchess County Society – Franklin D. Roosevelt and William P. Adams -- had joined the historical society. The men of Dutchess

County might have been perfectly willing to travel to the city to glorify the county's history, but the transplants didn't seem much interested in reciprocating. The only known reference to cooperation between the Dutchess County Society and the Dutchess County Historical Society is detailed in the 1919 volume of the Historical Society's Yearbook. Their joint project, which was to be funded with $250 from the New York City Society, was to reset or replace early highway milestones.

The Most Famous Member: Franklin Delano Roosevelt

The Dutchess County Society in The City of New York's most famous member was undoubtedly Franklin Delano Roosevelt. The future President was sent an application for membership in the Society on November 15, 1910, just one week after his election to the New York State Senate.[21] His application was accepted on November 28th of that same year.[22] The records at the Franklin D. Roosevelt Presidential Library show little involvement by Roosevelt in the Society until 1916 when he was serving as the Assistant Secretary of the Navy. On November 17, 1916 W.S. Cross wrote to Roosevelt and informed him that he had been elected President of the Society.[23] Roosevelt seemed to become immediately involved in the business of the Society and, on December 7 of that year, he wrote to W.S. Cross, Esq. conveying his attempt to get the President, the Vice President, or a cabinet member to attend the annual dinner.[24] Two weeks later on December 22, Roosevelt sent an invitation to The Honorable James Hamilton Lewis (a Democratic Senator from Illinois and a noted orator), inviting him to the upcoming Society banquet to be held on January 20 at

Figure 4. *Plaque dedicated to the young men who died in World War I. The text on the plaque reads: "Victory: 1917-1918. In Affectionate Memory of those Sons of Dutchess who made the Supreme Sacrifice that Democracy might Live, this tablet is presented by the Dutchess County Society in The City of New York." The Albert M. Rosenblatt Dutchess County Court House, Market Street, Poughkeepsie, NY. Photograph by Will Tatum.*

the Hotel Astor. Roosevelt called the dinner "one of the most important of the big dinners held in New York during each winter." [25] Secretary Cross continued corresponding with Roosevelt during the month of January, sharing his desire to settle on the speaker for the dinner. In a letter dated January 7, 1917, Cross shared that the dinner would have a nautical theme and requested an autographed photo and a cut of the official flag. He also indicated that he was looking for illustrations of battle ships. The dinner was to be "A Navy Night." [26]

In 1921, Roosevelt was appointed to serve on a committee charged with making arrangements for the erection and dedication of a memorial tablet on the Court House in Poughkeepsie to honor those who had died during World War I. The tablet can still be seen on the Market Street facade of the building (Figure 4).

Roosevelt's last major involvement with the Society prior to his contraction of poliomelytis in the summer of 1921 appears to have been his speech before the Society at their annual banquet on February 12, 1921. He was invited to speak again in 1936, this time as the President of the United States. [27] At the 1937 dinner, which celebrated the 40th Anniversary of the Society, a fund was raised for the Warm Springs Foundation. Roosevelt's responsibilities as President during the Depression and the war years severely hampered his ability to participate in the activities of the society. Still, society members valued him as a fellow son of Dutchess and their affection for him was conveyed via a February 25, 1942, letter from Walter D. Hoag, President of the Society.[28]

> The Hon. Franklin D. Roosevelt
> The White House
> Washington, D.C.
>
> Dear Mr. President,
> No formal note regarding the Dutchess County Society dinner at
> the Yale Club on the twenty-sixth was sent to you, knowing full
> well that you had more weighty subjects on your mind.We do
> want to express to you, however, the fact that at the dinner we
> will be thinking of your great effort to bring forth the virility of
> the American people.
>
> > Respectfully yours,
> > President of the Society

While Roosevelt was obviously no longer able to engage actively in the Dutchess County Society in The City of New York, his local friends still related to him as one of their own. A little over three years later, he would be dead, but his involvement with them would always be a treasured memory.

The Banquets

Winter in New York City at the turn of the twentieth century was filled with dazzling balls, nights out at the opera, and special dinners. So it was therefore not surprising that, within three months of their first meeting, the organizers of the Dutchess County Society held their first banquet. While the historical record is incomplete, the aforementioned note to President Roosevelt attests to the fact that these dinners continued, probably uninterrupted until at least 1942 (Figure 5). The membership application form declared the annual banquets to be "largely attended and uniformly successful. They have taken place amid the elegant surrounding of the finest hotels in New York City, and the list of post-prandial speakers includes many orators of national reputation." [29] Guests attending the banquets received multi-page programs that included the menu, and lists of speakers, officers, and banquet committee members.

The first banquet was held in the Murray Hill Hotel in 1897. Opened in 1884, the massive six hundred room hotel was located on Park Avenue and stretched from 40th to 41st Streets. An entrance for ladies on 40th Street

Figure 5. *Banquet of the Dutchess County Society in the City of New York at the Hotel Astor, January 15, 1910. Collection of the Franklin D. Roosevelt Library.*

provided a less public entry for females. The prime location was central to all the fashionable residential sections of the city and near to New York's Railroad Depot. Two large dining rooms were on the main floor and *The New York Times* reported that "they are the most elegantly furnished with carved oak chairs, upholstered in stamped leather, with Wilton carpets, silk velvet hangings in old gold on the walls, and the most exquisite frescoings."[30] Subsequent banquets during the first twenty-five years of the organization were held at equally elegant and fashionable hotels such as the Hotel Astor, the Waldorf Astoria, Delmonico's, the St. Regis, the Hotel Knickerbocker, and the Hotel Plaza. In later years, they moved to locations such as the Yale Club and the National Republican Club.

Wherever the banquet occurred, there was certain to be an elaborate dinner with as many as ten different courses. Bowing to the preferences of New York society at the time, the food and the menu were both French. The January 30, 1915, annual banquet at the Hotel Astor is a superb example of a typical repast. Dinner began with Cape Cod oysters, then moved on to duck in a Bordelaise sauce, followed by olives, celery and salted nuts. The three main entrees were sautéed shad, lamb mignons and Virginia ham timbales. A sorbet au Prunelle made with a sloe-flavored French liqueur was offered to cleanse the palate for the guinea fowl and tomatoes. Dessert featured a *ruche d'abeilles en surprise* and miniature pastries. After dinner beverage choices included G. H. Mumm's extra dry or cordon rouge champagne, Sanderson's Mountain Dew Scotch or White Rock sparkling water. Table guests were also offered the finest Egyptian cigarettes and imported Cuban cigars and cigarritos.[31]

The theme for the March 15, 1911 dinner at Astor House was atypical and much more whimsical. It featured Wappingers Oysters with Webatuck Sauce, Tyrell Lake Turtle Soup, Willowbrook Smelts Fried with Clove Sauce, Poughquag Potatoes, Shekomeko Sweetbreads, Pleasant Plains Peas, Roast Cokertown Squab, Hackensack Hominy, Rock City Salad, and a Basket of Stormville Strawberries.[32] Certainly a feast that the men of Dutchess could appreciate.

The Speakers and Banquet Entertainment

Another major component of the annual banquets was the presentation of remarks and responses to toasts. Often as many as six men were asked to participate in what must have been a lengthy part of the evening program. Occasionally a speech was delivered that focused on some aspect of Dutchess County history, but far more common were those that dealt with the politics of the day. Alfred T. Ackert, one of the founders of the Society, spoke on "Dutchess County in Colonial Times" at the second annual banquet on March 1, 1898, but his remarks were certainly overshadowed by those made by Justice Augustus Van Wyck. The dinner took place just after the February 15 sinking of the Maine in Havana Harbor and Van Wyck audaciously said:

> if the bullfrogs of a Latin nation want to plunge into our pond with a chunk-a-chunk the grand old bullfrogs of Dutchess, without any Hidalgoism, will sing that familiar song, "When I walk dat levee round, I'm looking for dat bully, he must be found."[33]

At the March 31, 1900 dinner, the featured speaker was Tunis Bergen, the President of the Holland Society. Van Bergen's topic was "Who Owns Civilization" and he expressed his opinion that France stood at the head of the civilized world.[34]

The January 12, 1906, banquet took place at Delmonico's and the highlight of the evening was the presentation of a bronze statuette of Samuel F. B. Morse to Sir Caspar Purdon Clarke, the British director of the Metropolitan Museum. After accepting the statuette, which was to be placed in the museum, Clarke went on to make a confession to the men of Dutchess.

> You may hiss me if you will. I was sent by a British millionaire once to this country to report on the colleges for the education of young women. I investigated Vassar and found it too aristocratic for me. [There were some hisses, soon silenced.] Wellesley exactly suited my idea of the college my millionaire friend wished to establish in England. I have freed my soul of this confession in the proper company and I feel better for it.[35]

Clarke's remarks did not go over well and over the next several days he was called upon to explain himself.

Elected officials were commonly invited to be featured speakers during the banquets. Most couldn't resist the temptation of appearing before four to five hundred men of high social standing and influence. Former Senator Warner Miller spoke on "Home Rule" in 1904. New York's Lieutenant Governor, Lewis Stuyvesant Chanler, was the guest of honor in 1908, followed by Governor Hughes in 1910 and Governor Dix in 1911. On January 17, 1914, eight months before the beginning of World War I, then Assistant Secretary of the Navy Franklin D. Roosevelt, spoke about American military preparedness. A *New York Times* article published the following day quoted him as saying that the "Navy is Overrated."[36]

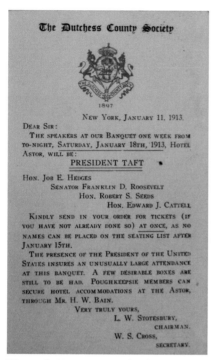

The January 18, 1913, banquet attracted more than 700 members to the grand ballroom of the Hotel Astor (Figure 6). Many undoubtedly came to hear President Taft who was scheduled to speak at 10:30 p.m. After much speculation and several incorrect reports about when the President would arrive, the diners finally gave up and went home shortly after midnight. The next day, the *New York Times* reported that Taft had been seen entering the Waldorf-Astoria for a Cornell dinner. [37]

Figure 6. *Announcement for the banquet featuring President Taft as the speaker, 1913. Collection of the Franklin D. Roosevelt Library.*

Given that the Dutchess County Society was a gentleman's club, it is not surprising that women did not often participate in the banquets. Reports of the 1912 banquet revealed that "two hundred ladies were in the boxes to listen and applaud" the presentations.[38] The twenty-eighth annual banquet on January 19, 1924, was remarkable in that Mrs. Vincent Astor "made one of her first talks on political topics," saying that "politicians make a mistake in trumping up issues for women." She went on to say that "Women, exhilarated by the privilege of suffrage and the prospect of office holding, have turned loose a good deal of foolishness on a patient world in the last few years, but they represent only a small minority."[39] Only one other woman was present at the dinner, while other ladies were allowed to hear the speakers from the ballroom balcony. Reportedly the men were paying close attention to her remarks.

The banquets were not all about ponderously heavy presentations. Mixed in with the speeches were light-hearted entertainment and frivolity. In 1911, the Hotel Astor ballroom was

lit only by faint lights displayed under the flower-bowls on each table and the hall was darkened while a searchlight was thrown on the American flag. During the dinner itself a man garbed as a Dutchess

County farmer lounged from table to table to express his horror at so much eating and drinking, and then the waiters, each wearing a Mexican peaked straw hat adorned with the blue, black and orange of the society's colors, marched in procession around the hall lighting their way with Japanese fireworks.[40]

The 1913 dinner featured a cabaret show, a boy singer, and a parade by the waiters dressed as farmers, and a young woman gowned in pink, who darted in and out among the diners as she sang. The most novel form of entertainment, however, occurred in 1922 when a search was undertaken for the prettiest girl in Dutchess County who would cook and serve doughnuts during the dinner.[41]

The Souvenirs

One of the highlights of the annual dinners was the presentation to attendees of a special souvenir to mark the occasion. The first souvenir was given at the first dinner on March 26, 1897. Barely three months had passed since the formation of the Society, and there was not enough time to commission something unique, so society leaders purchased small Beachcraft Jig Saw puzzles entitled "As The Sun Dips In The Golden Sea." The image on the puzzle, the famous "Witch Tree" at Pebble Beach, California, was a long way from Dutchess County but organizers pasted a paper label with the society's emblem and the words "Souvenir Dutchess County Society in the City of New York 1897" on the top and gave them to the assembled guests (Figures 7&8). In 1901, the souvenirs were paper imitations of Dutchess County logs with hollow receptacles in the middle in which ice cream was served.[42] Kerley Family records at the Dutchess County Historical Society indicate that the 1909 souvenir was a beige china mug with the Dutchess County seal and inscription and the 1910 souvenir was an embossed leather billfold with the Society's seal. A plaque bearing the arms of the Society was one of the souvenirs in 1911. Also known to have been given to Society members were small, engraved desktop clocks, pen,

Figure 7. *Souvenir puzzle box given out at the first annual banquet, 1897.*

Figure 8. *Souvenir jig-saw puzzle depicting the Pebble Beach Witch Tree, assembled from souvenir given out at the first annual banquet, 1897. Haight Family Collection.*

dishes, clips, thermos bottles, a porcelain trinket dish, a leather telephone number record book and engraved silver boxes.

The most popular and highly collectible society souvenirs were a series of blue and white Royal Doulton plates, each centered with an image of a different Dutchess County building surrounded by stylized tulips (Figure 10). The first plate, given out at the 1910 dinner, depicted the Van Kleeck House in Poughkeepsie. Four more plates were issued between 1911 and 1915 and featured Mt. Gulian in Beacon, the Old Dutch Church in Fishkill, the Kip-Beekman-Livingston House in Rhinebeck, the Henry Livingston House in Poughkeepsie, and the Mesier Homestead in Wappingers Falls. In February of 1915, members received a postcard (Figure 9). informing them that the 1910–1915 plates were available for purchase at $1.00 each. The card noted that it was the "last chance to complete a set as the balance

Figure 9. *Postcard sent to President Franklin D. Roosevelt regarding the purchase of souvenir plates. Note the simplicity of the address and the misspelling of his name. Collection of the Franklin D. Roosevelt Library.*

Figure 10. *Souvenir plate depicting the Old Dutch Church at Fishkill Village from annual banquet, 1912.Collection of the Dutchess County Historical Society.*

are to be destroyed to enhance the value of the complete sets."[43] In 1917, a seventh plate was issued to "complete the set";[44] it featured the First Collegiate School in Poughkeepsie. Another postcard that was sent to promote the banquet and the plate pronounced the plate was "For the Home. For the Office. A beautiful, useful article of merit and value. Something you'll use daily."[45]

There has been much speculation about why no plate seems to have been issued in 1916. One unsubstantiated story is that a plate was produced but lost at sea when the ship that was transporting the order was sunk. The more likely explanation is tied to the failure of the company that was the importer of the plates. Higgins and Seiter was one of the best known and oldest china and glass emporiums in New York City, having been established just after the end of the Civil War by Col. Charles Jacob Seiter and brothers Barton B. and Arthur Higgins.Col. Charles J. Seiter was the first Vice-President of the Society Council in 1910, the year the first plate was issued. The 1912--1915 plates are all marked Higgins and Seiter on the reverse of the plate. The company, already weakened by some financial difficulties, was forced into bankruptcy early in 1915 when the war in Europe made it impossible to import fine china and glassware. These circumstances may have resulted in there being no plate for 1916. Within the curatorial records for the photographic collection at the FDR Presidential Library there is a reference to a photograph of a sepia and white woven silk picture of the Poughkeepsie Collegiate School. The background for the photograph states it was presented as a souvenir at the society's annual dinner at the Hotel Astor on January 22, 1916. The following year at the January 10, 1917, dinner, the last known plate was issued and it too depicted the Collegiate School.

The Mystery of the Society

Although collectors of Dutchess County memorabilia have long been familiar with the souvenir plates and banquet programs and menu cards, little about the society itself has been known. Were it not for the collections housed at the Presidential Library in Hyde Park, New York and *The New*

York Times Archives, this story could not be told. Attempts to locate other material related to the history of the society in such places as the New York Historical Society, the Museum of the City of New York, and the New York Public Library have all proven to be fruitless. Clearly the society was still in existence as late as November 15, 1944, when a postcard was mailed to FDR announcing the Forty-eighth Dinner at the National Republican Club.[46] Five months later the President was dead. Thus ended his files on the society.

What happened to this robust and vibrant organization is not known, but a poem on the cover of the 1931 Membership List booklet attests to the love of Dutchess County that had given birth to and sustained the organization throughout is existence.[47]

> "On Fair Dutchess my memory lingers
> With joyful Thoughts of long ago,
> Awakening within me happy visions
> Of beauteous hills magnifico;
> Of friendships formed in days gone by
> Through many years enduring,
> Of gladsome times in the Old Home Town,
> With memories and recollections alluring."

---

[1] "The Holland Society of New York – History of the Society," <http://hollandsociety. com/history.html

[2] The author's interest in the Dutchess County Society in The City of New York was sparked by recent donations of souvenir plates to the Dutchess County Historical Society.

[3] Membership List, Historical Sketch, 1931; Folder: Dutchess County Society in the City of New York; Interdepartmental Correspondence, 1913 – 1920; Papers As Secretary of the Navy; Franklin D. Roosevelt Library, Hyde Park, New York. I did much of the research for this paper at the Franklin D. Roosevelt Library in Hyde Park, New York. I would like to thank the Library for the opportunity to conduct research there. Please note that citations for reference to materials held in the Franklin D. Roosevelt Presidential Library in Hyde Park, New York, follow the format suggested by the Library: specific description, date and nature of the document, the folder title, the series (groupings of documents), the collection, and finally the institution. For purposes of these endnotes, after the first citation within a specific series, subsequent series identifications are identified as ASN for Assistant Secretary of the Navy; FBPA for Family, Business and Personal Affairs; PPF for President's Personal File; and VF for Vertical File. The collection and the institution are the same for all citations and will not be repeated.

[4] Application For Membership, The Dutchess County Society in the City of New York, n.d. ("191..," printed on upper right corner, see Figure 2, therefore, postdates 1910); Haight Family Collection.

[5] Membership List, Historical Sketch, 1931; Folder: Dutchess County Society in the City of New York; ASN.

[6] "New Development In Club Life, Recent Organization of Numerous State and County Societies in This City," *The New York Times*, February 16, 1902.

[7] Ibid.

[8] "Dutchess County Society Reunion," *The New York Times*, December 5, 1901.

[9] "New Development In Club Life, Recent Organization of Numerous State and County Societies in This City," The New York Times, February 16, 1902.

[10] *The Home County Magazine*, Vol. II, No. 1, August 1923; Periodicals; Franklin D. Roosevelt Library, Hyde Park, New York.

[11] Application For Membership, The Dutchess County Society in the City of New York, n.d. ("191..," printed on upper right corner, see Figure 2, therefore, postdates 1910); Haight Family Collection.

[12] Letter, Carl Griffen to Franklin D. Roosevelt, February 2, 1940; Folder: Dutchess County Society in the City of New York; President's Personal File; Franklin D. Roosevelt Library, Hyde Park, New York.

[13] "Dr. Kerley's Estate Grosses $1,638,292, *The Poughkeepsie New Yorker*, February 13, 1947.

[14] Kerley Family and Roger Leonard Folders held by the Historic Red Hook organization, The Elmendorph Inn, Red Hook, New York.

[15] "Justice Alfred T. Ackert," *The New York Times*, April 5, 1875.

[16] "Alfred T. Ackert," *The New York Times*, June 20, 1873.

[17] "Justice Alfred T. Ackert," *The New York Times*, April 5, 1875.

[18] "J. Walter Righter's Funeral Today," *The New York Times*, August 2, 1927.

[19] *Transactions of The Homeopathic Medical Society of the State of New York For the Year 1903*, page 27.

[20] Annual Membership Lists, Vertical File; Dutchess County Society in the City of New York; Franklin D. Roosevelt Library, Hyde Park, New York.

[21] Letter, E. Lyman Brown To Franklin D. Roosevelt, November 15, 1910; Folder: Dutchess County Society in the City of New York; ASN.

[22] Membership Certificate of Franklin D. Roosevelt, November 28, 1910; Folder: Dutchess County Society in the City of New York; ASN.

[23] Letter, W.S. Cross to Franklin D. Roosevelt, November 17, 1916; Folder: Dutchess County Society in the City of New York; ASN.

[24] Letter, Franklin D. Roosevelt to W.S. Cross, December 7, 1916; Folder: Dutchess County Society in the City of New York; ASN.

[25] Letter, Franklin D. Roosevelt to the Honorable James Hamilton Lewis, December 22, 1916; Folder: Dutchess County Society in the City of New York; ASN.

[26] Letter, W. S. Cross to Franklin D. Roosevelt, January 7, 1917; Folder: Dutchess County Society in the City of New York; ASN.

[27] Letter, Lewis E. Christian to Franklin D. Roosevelt, December 4, 1935; Folder: Dutchess County Society in the City of New York; PPF.

[28] Letter, Walter D. Hoag to Franklin D. Roosevelt, February 25, 1942; Folder: Dutchess County Society in the City of New York; PPF.

[29] Application For Membership, The Dutchess County Society in the City of New York, n.d. ("191..," printed on upper right corner, see Figure 2, therefore, postdates 1910); Haight Family Collection.

[30] "The Lost 1884 Murray Hill Hotel—Park Avenue and 40th Street," http://daytoninmanhattan.blogspot.com.

[31] Program Booklet, "The Dutchess County Society in the City of New York," 19th Annual Banquet," January 30, 1915, Vertical File; Dutchess County Society in the City of New York.

[32] Program Booklet, "The Dutchess County Society in the City of New York, 15th Annual Banquet," March 15, 1911, Vertical File; Dutchess County Society in the City of New York.

[33] "Dutchmen Show Patriotism, Preeminent Men Speak At the Annual Banquet of the Dutchess County Society," *The New York Times*, March 1, 1898.

[34] "What Is Doing In Society, Dutchess County Society Dinner," *The New York Times*, March 31, 1900.

[35] "Sir C. Purdon Clarke Not Taking Everything," *The New York Times*, January 13, 1906.

[36] "Navy Is Overrated Says F.D. Roosevelt," *The New York Times*, January 18, 1914.

[37] "Dutchess Men Dine," and "Taft At Beth-el To-Day," *The New York Times*, January 19, 1913.

[38] "Dutchess Countymen Dine," *The New York Times*, February 4, 1912.

[39] "Mrs. Vincent Astor Speaks On Politics," *The New York Times*, January 20, 1924.

[40] "Dutchess County Men Dine, Many Novel Features Enliven Their Annual Feast," *The New York Times*, January 15, 1911.

[41] "Prettiest Doughnut Cooker Wanted For Dutchess Dinner," *The New York Times*, December 11, 1922.

[42] "Sons of Dutchess County, Gen. Wheeler Is their Guest of Honor At Annual Dinner," The New York Times, March 2, 1901.

[43] Postcard, Dutchess County Society in New York City to Franklin D. Roosevelt, February 6, 1915, Folder: Dutchess County Society in New York City; Papers Pertaining to Family, Business and Personal Affairs.

[44] Postcard, Dutchess County Society in New York City to Franklin D. Roosevelt, January 11, 1917, Folder: Dutchess County Society in New York City; FBPA.

[45] Ibid.

[46] Postcard, Dutchess County Society in the City of New York to Franklin D. Roosevelt, November 15, 1944, PPF.

[47] Membership List, Dutchess County Society in the City of New York, 1931, Vertical File, Dutchess County Society in the City of New York.

"Of Some Definite Historic Value": FDR and the Preservation of History

by Bob Clark

On December 10, 1938, President Franklin D. Roosevelt called the press into the Oval Office and announced to them his intention to build the nation's first presidential library on land carved from the Roosevelt estate in Hyde Park, Dutchess County, New York. He had been considering the plan for some time, and he had drawn his first sketch (Figure 1) of the future library on April 12, 1937 – less than three months after being sworn in to his second term as president.[1]

Franklin Roosevelt was unique among the pantheon of presidents in many ways, but particularly in the volume of books, official and personal papers, memorabilia, and historic manuscripts he had accumulated during his life.

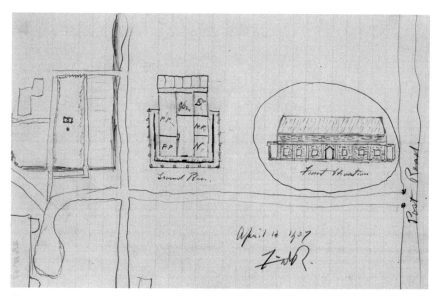

Figure 1. *Franklin Roosevelt's original sketch of his presidential library to be built on land carved from the Roosevelt Estate in Hyde Park, New York. FDR Library Significant Documents Collection.*

FDR's Commitment to Dutchess County
and the History of the Hudson Valley

In founding the nation's first presidential library, President Roosevelt sought to establish an institution unlike any other in America. Not only did he want the Library to house and make available to the American people the records of his presidency, but also he wanted to help preserve the wonderful culture and traditions of New York's Hudson Valley, and in particular his own home county of Dutchess.

Indeed, at his press conference announcing the library project, he made a special point to call out his local history collections:

> ...I have also two rather specialized collections which are of some definite historic value: a collection of paintings, drawing, prints, manuscript letters and documents, log-books, pamphlets and books relating to the American sailing Navy from 1775 to date; and a smaller collection of similar material relating to the Hudson River, and especially Dutchess County and the town of Hyde Park. These collections would be placed in the proposed building, together with the public papers, etc.[2]

From boyhood, the Hudson Valley's history and diverse culture fascinated Roosevelt. He studied the histories of his colonial ancestors, the larger Dutch influence on the Hudson Valley, the impact of the other river families on the area, and the traditions of the Hudson Valley's native peoples. He collected books, historic manuscripts, and artifacts of the valley, and his expansive collection helped inspire FDR's desire that his new presidential library also be a center for the study of Dutchess County and the Hudson Valley region.[3]

FDR's Hudson Valley and Dutchess County collection includes correspondence, diaries, genealogical notebooks, account ledgers, indentures, receipts and other business records, scrapbooks, and assorted other miscellany.[4] The collection contains materials documenting prominent Hudson Valley families, such as the Beekmans, the DePeysters, the DuBoises, the Livingstons, the Quackenbushes, and the Van Wycks, as well as communities and organizations like the Hyde Park Drug Store, St. James Episcopal Church in Hyde Park, St. Peter's Episcopal Church in Rhinebeck, Dutchess Turnpike Company, genealogical notebooks compiled from various cemetery records and private family collections, the Coxsackie Town Record of Freeborn Slaves, and records of the Town of New Paltz. These extensive materials date back as early as the year 1540, and they inspired Franklin Roosevelt to become an active local historian. FDR was named historian for the Town of Hyde Park in 1926 and served until 1931, when he resigned because of the press of his duties as Governor of New York. He also was an avid participant in many other historical organizations and collector societies.[5]

FDR and the Dutchess County Historical Society

Naturally, Roosevelt was a leading member of the Dutchess County Historical Society, having joined the organization in 1914. Although Roosevelt was not one of the founding or organizing members, he is recorded as having joined in the first year of the Society's existence.[6] He led meetings at the Roosevelt home known as *Springwood*, and gave lectures on local history to the group. He was appointed to the Society's first Membership Committee in 1923 (Figure 2).[7] Even after his election as president of the United States in 1932, FDR continued to write and compile major local history publications for the Society, and he still found time to meet with its members when he visited Hyde Park.[8] In 1929, Roosevelt wrote an introduction to the book, *Dutch Houses in the Hudson Valley Before 1776*, authored by his good friend in the Society, Miss Helen Wilkinson Reynolds.[9] In 1940, Roosevelt edited the volume, *Records of Crum Elbow Precinct, Dutchess County, New York, 1738–1761*.[10] Clearly, FDR's interest in the Dutchess County Historical Society was lasting even through years when he was Governor of the State of New York or was in Washington, D.C. serving as president. At the Dutchess County Historical Society, Roosevelt accepted the position of Vice President for the Town of Hyde Park, a post he held from 1926 until his death in 1945. At that time, the Yearbook published a memorial portrait of their member and president of the United States.[11]

Figure 2. *Dutchess County Historical Society leadership at Springwood during 1927 pilgrimage to Hyde Park. Left to right: John J. Mylod, trustee; Helen Wilkinson Reynolds, trustee; William Platt Adams, president; Eleanor Roosevelt; Franklin D. Roosevelt, vice-president. Photograph from Wide World Photos. Collection of Dutchess County Historical Society.*

In his earliest designs of his presidential library (Figure 1), he specifically designated a special "Dutchess County Room" where the Society could meet, maintain its collections, and display items to the public. Although used as a conference room by Library staff today, the Dutchess County Room was restored back to its original colors and condition during the Library's 2010–2013 renovation.

Projects in Dutchess County Initiated by Roosevelt

Roosevelt also selected the Dutch Colonial style and the regional field-stone for the Library's exterior. If you tour New Deal era public buildings throughout the Hudson Valley, including the Rhinebeck Post Office, the Hyde Park Post Office, the Haviland Middle School in Hyde Park, and the Poughkeepsie Post Office, you will see the influence of Roosevelt's beloved Dutch Colonial style in their design.[12] In another example of Roosevelt's interest in American culture and Dutchess County's history, the President was instrumental in acquiring the Vanderbilt Mansion in Hyde Park for the National Park Service, rightly believing it to be the only completely intact example of America's Gilded Age lifestyle.[13]

And, of course, it was FDR who became the first president to plan for the posthumous transfer of his own home to the government. Roosevelt knew that the American people longed to learn more about the childhood and everyday life of its leaders—part of our democracy's own unique style of local history. The Home of Franklin D. Roosevelt National Historic Site was opened to the American people on April 12, 1946—just one year after the President's death.[14]

FDR's Interest in the National Cultural Heritage

But FDR's commitment to preserving the nation's historical and cultural heritage spread well beyond the borders of Dutchess County and the banks of the Hudson River.

As Roosevelt campaigned for the presidency in 1932, the nation grappled with a staggering unemployment rate of 25%, a collapsing banking system, and a loss of faith in American democracy. Roosevelt faced these challenges head-on. During the campaign and in his First Inaugural Address, FDR declared his intentions to use "bold, persistent experimentation" and "action, and action now" to put people back to work and reform government through a series of programs that were known as the New Deal.

FDR announced the creation of the Works Progress Administration in a Fireside Chat on April 28, 1935. "Our responsibility," the President declared, "is to all of the people in this country. This is a great national crusade to destroy enforced idleness which is an enemy of the human spirit generated by this depression."[15] He also told Congress in 1935 that "We must preserve not only the bodies of the unemployed but also their self-respect, their self-reliance and courage and determination."[16]

To implement this far reaching mission, FDR turned to Harry Hopkins—one of the most creative, energetic enemies of red tape the government has ever seen. The WPA immediately set about allocating billions of dollars to infrastructure projects such as roads, dams, bridges, airports and government buildings such as courthouses and schools. By January 1936, 2.8 million people would be on the WPA payroll.[17]

But Hopkins was not just an efficient administrator. He had a background in liberal arts, was a social worker by training, and had a great respect for the arts and artists. He saw the need not only to build the country's physical infrastructure but to preserve and advance its culture and history as well—all of its history and culture, in all of its forms, and from all of its locations. In the summer of 1935, he announced the establishment of the WPA's Federal One project – a multi-part project to employ visual artists, musicians, writers, historians, archivists, and theatre workers. When criticized for using government money for such purposes, Hopkins famously responded: "Hell, they've got to eat just like other people!"[18]

The first component of Federal One, the Federal Art Project, was given the task of taking artists from the relief rolls and putting them to work. This required creating opportunities for every level of artistic ability, both traditional artists and those in emerging styles that had yet to gain wide acceptance, such as Cubism and Expressionism.

When we think of "New Deal Art," most of us think of the murals (Figure3). For all the support for new and emerging styles, it was this representational art that took the greatest hold. These murals depict the origins, trials, and progress of America and were painted by the WPA in schools, libraries, city halls, hospitals, airports and colleges. And the necessary underlying material—blank walls—were available everywhere and therefore accessible to artists in every location around the country.

Historical murals in many of these buildings reflect the traditions and history of the localities. Indeed, a guiding principle of public building projects throughout the country was that the new buildings and the public art within them should capture the history, spirit, and artistic traditions of the particular regions.[19] In the Rhinebeck and Hyde Park Post Offices, for example, murals painted by the Hudson Valley artist Olin Dows depict scenes of Native Americans, Dutch explorers and settlers, prominent citizens, and important events and locations in the histories of those communities.[20]

Ultimately, the Federal Art Project would produce almost 475,000 works of art. But perhaps the Project's most important and enduring contribution to American cultural memory came in the form of the Index of American Design, an effort that employed researchers, artists and photographers to compile an exact pictorial record of the things that Americans had lived, worked and played with since the 1700s. Index workers fanned out across the country locating examples of costume, furniture, pottery, metalwork, and folk art. They photographed, drew or painted the objects, and documented them in minute detail. The result was an index of 22,000 images and descriptions depicting the breadth of American Design.[21]

Another component of Federal One was the Federal Writers Project. It is perhaps best known for producing the American Guide Series. Inspired by the famous and indispensable Baedecker international guidebooks published in Germany, the Project envisioned a series of guidebooks produced for each state as well as for major cities. They would not only employ writers to produce them, but also hopefully increase tourism in those areas. The guides would contain well researched essays on the state's history, geology, ecology and cultural scene, as well as give detailed descriptions of towns, city neighborhoods, monuments, natural wonders, and other highlights. Finally, carefully designed and mapped tours would give the readers the ability to discover each state's magic for themselves.

Ultimately, the Project produced an enduring series of guidebooks that revealed America's multilayered culture. The guides did not shirk from describing African-American or Hispanic culture, or from pointing out injustices or the living conditions of the poor. Archivists dug into the history of each location, and some of the nation's most promising writers composed the essays that accompanied the narrative descriptions.

When the American Guides began appearing in print in 1937, they received outstanding reviews from literary critics. The guide to New York State was published in late 1940, and it described the Hudson River as "that spacious and magnificent fiord." It continued, "To say that any river route is incomparable in beauty may, of course, be extravagant, but there is nothing like it in the United States, at least, and Yorkers feel a thankful pride that this impressive scenery is included in their varied homeland."[22]

An important sub-project of the Federal One program was the Folklore Division that sought to gather American folklore in all its forms, from ex-slave narratives in Florida, to accounts of riding the rails by hoboes, to Bahamian and Spanish immigrant music, to Appalachian hillbilly music, to tall tales in Texas, to the black experience in Harlem. The goal was to interview as many and as diverse a people as possible to create understanding and to improve people's lives. Today the recordings made by the Folklore Division are housed at the Library of Congress.

In all, the Writers Project produced over 275 full-length books, 700 pamphlets and hundreds of Ex-Slave Narrative and Folklore recordings. The Project also employed archivists who studied local historical records and created finding aids and guides to those collections.[23] Indeed, Franklin Roosevelt's own collection of Hudson Valley and Dutchess county historical materials housed at the Roosevelt Library includes the WPA Historical Records Survey Project's Inventory of Dutchess County Records.[24]

The First Presidential Library – now the Franklin D. Roosevelt Presidential Library and Museum

The WPA arts projects – and indeed the New Deal itself – began to wane in the late 1930s. But at the same time, FDR was carrying on with the project that was a continuation of all these prior efforts to preserve and disseminate history, culture, and information among the people: the establishment of the first presidential library.

The Roosevelt Library itself is reflective of the fundamental shift in our national dialogue and our understanding of our relationship to our government and elected officials. We must remember that before FDR, there was no such thing as a presidential library. Indeed, before FDR there was no such thing as the National Archives. Although construction on a National Archives building had begun during Herbert Hoover's administration, there was no agency to go into it.

It was not until 1934 that FDR pushed through Congress the creation of the National Archives establishment and appointed the first Archivist of the United States. President Roosevelt had been appalled at how the records of the Federal government were being kept, and was intent on preserving important national records and making them accessible to the American people. So almost immediately, FDR involved himself in every aspect of the new agency's operation, from appointment of personnel, to organization of stack areas, to decisions on collection policy, to recommending new techniques for preservation such as microfilm.[25]

Out of this experience—as well as FDR's longtime interest in history—grew the idea of the presidential library (Figure 1). FDR was determined that his collections would not suffer the same fate as those of his predecessors which, if they survived at all, were often incomplete and difficult to find and use.

Figure 3. *In the final mural panel painted by Olin Dows in the Hyde Park Post Office, FDR is depicted in his car reviewing the building plans for a local construction project. FDR Library Photograph Collection.*

Franklin Roosevelt's library was to be built on sixteen acres on Roosevelt's own estate in Hyde Park. This not only made access convenient to the President but began decentralizing government records away from Washington and out into the country—an example that the National Archives follows to this day with its network of regional archives, records centers, and presidential libraries.

To take politics out of the equation, the Library building was built with private donations, not taxpayer dollars. Then the building, land and collections were donated to the National Archives to be staffed and maintained by impartial archives and museum professionals. This ingenious system of private finance and public maintenance was made permanent in the Presidential Libraries Act of 1955.

Figure 4. *President Franklin D. Roosevelt dedicates the Franklin D. Roosevelt Library in Hyde Park, New York, June 30, 1941. FDR Library Photograph Collection.*

On June 30, 1941—a warm, early summer day in Hyde Park—President Franklin D. Roosevelt stood at a podium in the courtyard of the newly completed Dutch colonial style building (Figure 4). As he addressed his gathered friends and neighbors, FDR dedicated his library as the "newest house in which people's records are preserved" and hoped

that millions of our citizens from every part of the land will be glad that what we do today makes available to future Americans the story of what we have lived and are living today, and what we will continue to live during the rest of our lives.[26]

Seventy-two years later, on June 30, 2013, the Franklin D. Roosevelt Presidential Library and Museum was rededicated following a three-year, $35 million renovation project that carefully retained the historical integrity of FDR's design, but that brought the building up to modern National Archives standards for collection access, preservation, and security.

New permanent exhibits were installed that tell the story of the Roosevelt presidency beginning in the depths of the Great Depression and continuing through the New Deal and World War II, with an emphasis on both Franklin and Eleanor Roosevelt's relationship with the American people. Special interactives, immersive audio-visual theaters, and rarely seen artifacts convey the dramatic story of the Roosevelt era. The exhibit concludes with a special "Behind the Scenes" area that makes it possible for visitors to get a special peek into the collections of the President and First Lady. Here, visitors can see FDR's model ship collection, his 1936 Ford Phaeton (with hand-controls), Val-Kill furniture, family portraits and Hudson River paintings, New Deal art, and gifts of state.

Today, the Roosevelt Library houses some seventeen million pages of archival materials in 400 distinct collections; over 50,000 books including Roosevelt's own personal library of 22,000 volumes; 150,000 audio-visual items; and 35,000 museum objects.

The Roosevelt Library also provides global access to its collections through its website, www.fdrlibrary.marist.edu. In December 2013, the Library launched a new digital repository and virtual research room called FRANKLIN that makes hundreds of thousands of digitized documents and photographs accessible to anyone, anywhere in the world.

When FDR dedicated the Library in June 1941, the world was aflame in war, and democracies everywhere were under siege by dictatorships. But for FDR, the building of a library in such a time was an "act of faith" in our own democracy. From the beginning, the Roosevelt Library's mission has been to make its collections accessible to all Americans so that they "can gain in judgment in creating their own future."[27]

---

[1] FDR's Sketch of the Franklin D. Roosevelt Library, April 12, 1937. Significant Documents Collection, Franklin D. Roosevelt Presidential Library (hereinafter FDRL).

[2] Franklin D. Roosevelt, 508th Press Conference, December 10, 1938, *Public Papers and Addresses of Franklin D. Roosevelt, 1938 Volume: The Continuing Struggle for Liberalism* (New York: Macmillan, 1941), p. 632.

[3] Introduction to finding aid to FDR's Hudson River Valley and Dutchess County Manuscript Collection, FDRL.

[4] Ibid.

[5] Ibid. For more information on FDR's Hudson River and Dutchess County Manuscript Collection, see John C. Ferris, "Franklin D. Roosevelt: His Development and Accomplishments as a Local Historian," *Dutchess County Historical Society Yearbook - 1983*, Vol. 68, pp.17-39.

[6] Franklin Delano Roosevelt is listed as a member in the first year along with approximately 400 others. Clearly, he was not present at the organizing meetings for the Society. *Year Book of the Dutchess County Historical Society*, May 1914--April 1915, p.31.

[7] " Minutes of the Semi-Annual Meeting, Oct 18th, 1923," *Year Book, Dutchess County Historical Society*, 1924, p.7. The president of the Society appointed ten people to the committee including Miss Helen Wilkinson Reynolds, Mr. John J. Mylod, and Mr. J. Willis Reese.

[8] Ferris, "FDR-Local Historian," pp. 26, 30-34.

[9] Helen Wilkinson Reynolds (with an introduction by Franklin D. Roosevelt), *Dutch Houses in The Hudson Valley Before 1776* (Prepared under the Auspices of The Holland Society of New York) (New York: Payson and Clarke Ltd., 1929).

[10] Franklin D. Roosevelt, ed., *Records of Crum Elbow Precinct, Dutchess County, New York, 1738--1761* (Poughkeepsie, New York: Collections of The Dutchess County Historical Society, Vol VII, 1940).

[11] See Reproduction of painting by Frank O. Salisbury, Franklin Delano Roosevelt, Yearbook, Dutchess County Historical Society, Vol. 30, 1945. opposite p. 20. For information on the Hon Franklin Delano Roosevelt as Vice President for the Town of Hyde Park, see Year Books of the Dutchess County Historical Society for the years 1926-1944. The main officers of the organization were augmented by Vice Presidents representing each of twenty-two towns (including the City of Poughkeepsie and the City of Beacon).

[12] Cynthia M. Koch and Lynn Bassanese, "Roosevelt and His Library", *Prologue* 33 (Summer 2001): pp. 78.

[13] See President's Official File 6-P: Department of the Interior: National Park Service: Vanderbilt Mansion, FDRL.

[14] See President's Official File 6-P: Department of the Interior: National Park Service: FDR Home, FDRL.

[15] Franklin D. Roosevelt, The First Fireside Chat of 1935, April 28, 1935, *Public Papers and Addresses of Franklin D. Roosevelt, 1935 Volume: The Court Disapproves* (New York: Random house, 1938), p. 136.

[16] Franklin D. Roosevelt, Annual Message to Congress, January 4, 1935, *Public Papers and Addresses of Franklin D. Roosevelt, 1935 Volume: The Court Disapproves* (New York: Random house, 1938), p.20.

[17] Nick Taylor, American-Made: Then Enduring Legacy of the WPA: When FDR Put the Nation to Work (New York: Bantam Books, 2008), p. 220.

[18] Susan Quinn, Furious Improvisation: How the WPA and a Cast of Thousands Made High Art Out of Desperate Times (New York: Walker & Company, 2008), p. 11.

[19] See Taylor, *American-Made*, pp. 270-277.

[20] Ferris, "FDR-Local Historian," p. 24.

[21] See Taylor, American-Made, pp. 278-279.

[22] Federal Writer's Program, Works Projects Administration, *New York: A Guide to the Empire State* (New York: Oxford University Press, 1940), p. 8

[23] For an in-depth study of the Federal Writer's Project, see David A. Taylor, *Soul of a People: The WPA Writer's Project Uncovers Depression America* (Hoboken: John Wiley & Sons, 2009).

[24] Ferris, "FDR-Local Historian," pp. 34-35.

[25] See Bob Clark, "FDR, Archivist: The Shaping of the National Archives", *Prologue* 38 (Winter2006): pp. 42-47

[26] Franklin D. Roosevelt, Remarks at the Dedication of the Franklin D. Roosevelt Library at Hyde Park, New York, June 30, 1941, *Public Papers and Addresses of Franklin D. Roosevelt, 1941 Volume: The Call to Battle Stations* (New York: Harper & Brothers, 1950), p. 249.

[27] Ibid., p. 248.

Arthur Tompkins Benson:
Early Member of the
Dutchess County Historical Society

by Caroline Rogers Reichenberg
Co-Historian, Town of Dover,
President, Town of Dover Historical Society, Inc.

Arthur T. Benson was the first person from Dover to become a member of the Dutchess County Historical Society. According to the records of the Dutchess County Historical Society, Benson became a member shortly after the founding of the organization in April, 1914. He is listed as a member in 1915, the second year of the organization's existence. The listing records him as "Arthur T. Benson—Dover Plains." At that time, 199 members were recorded.[1] This brief account of Arthur Benson may afford us a view of one of the early members of the society—perhaps even a typical member—an individual who was well educated and dedicated to history, a writer whose first occupation—farming—was entirely practical. He was someone interested in history primarily in order to research and preserve his family genealogy. He was a farmer, an educated man who taught school, kept a journal, and wrote poetry.

Mr. Benson (1860-1931) lived in the north east part of Dover Plains. He named Dover as the location of his farm; in fact, it was in the Town of Amenia. This was the same land that his father, grandfather and great grandfather, the pioneer Jacob Benson, had once settled.

In the winter of 1880, Mr. Benson was a teacher in the one-room school house on East Mountain with sixteen registered students. His writings tell us that was his first experience of teaching. His salary was $2.00 per week and board. He remarked that he boarded at a place for two weeks. Mr. Benson commented that

> the hospitality was unexcelled; cuisine above criticism; and big feather
> beds an invitation to calm repose, undisturbed by the Wintery blasts
> that sweep over the mountain.[2]

Mr. Benson married Kate Clark Bartlett in 1890; they had seven children.

In August 1914, the Benson family held a reunion at the house of Mrs. Carmel G. Benson and her son Frank D. Benson in Dover Plains with about seventy-five family members present. Short addresses were given by several members including Arthur T. Benson. The A. Benson Family Association was formed of which Arthur T. Benson was elected President.[3]

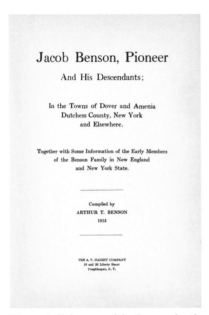

Jacob Benson, Pioneer

And His Descendants;

In the Towns of Dover and Amenia
Dutchess County, New York
and Elsewhere.

Together with Some Information of the Early Members
of the Benson Family in New England
and New York State.

Compiled by
ARTHUR T. BENSON
1915

THE A. V. HAIGHT COMPANY
18 and 20 Liberty Street
Poughkeepsie, N. Y.

Figure 1. *Title page of the Benson family book: Arthur T. Benson (compiled by), Jacob Benson, Pioneer and His Descendants: In the Towns of Dover and Amenia, Dutchess County, New York and Elsewhere (Poughkeepsie, N.Y.: A.V. Haight Co., 1915).*

Arthur Benson was dedicated to preserving his heritage, so much so that he compiled the Benson family book in 1915, published by A.V. Haight Co., Poughkeepsie. NY.[4] The book of one hundred thirty pages includes material on Jacob Benson, pioneer, and his descendents. This book has been a treasure for the descendants in the Benson family as well as others interested in the history of Dover and Amenia. Many interesting facts and anecdotes in the Dover—Amenia area were included.

Mr. Benson also published his observations about life in Dover in newspaper articles. A news item he wrote was published in *The Sunday Courier*, November 12, 1922, focusing on the first and last people living on Preston Mountain in Dover. The value of that writing today is to give us a small window of information on the way of life for many of Dover's early settlers on land that was a part of the "Oblong," subject of a land dispute settled between New York and Connecticut. He reported that the last resident on the mountain lived a simple and uncomplicated life, caring for the cemetery on East Mountain, allowing bees to use the clapboards on his home as their beehive. Furthermore, Mr. Benson claimed that the last resident would not disturb a rattle snake while it was sunning its self on the house steps. He wrote of the man's kind hospitality to have offered Benson home-made root beer when the author stopped to visit him. Mr. Benson wrote of more memories from other descendants from the first settlers in the area. In his writing, he continued to mention information about a Tory Cave located on the mountain that had been used during the Revolutionary War.[5] .

He lived on his farm for many years before retiring to live with one of his daughters prior to his death in December 1931.[6]

Mr. Benson's Family Book concludes with the following poem he authored:[7]

RETRISPECTIVE

We boast no crest nor Knightly crown,
By tyrant's favor won
For darksome deeds of much renown;
In royal service done.

Ours but the common, bumble span,
In field and workshop spent,
The love of home and fellow-man,
Of duty and content.

The lonely rock-bound barren shore,
Where Pilgrim fathers tread,
Could offer nothing, then, much more,
Than scant supply of bread.

And freedom, too, of honest thought,
Was to their souls refused,
That liberty that they had sought,
Their leaders, stern, abused.

Chafed by the Puritanic reign,
That privilege denied,
Our fathers ventured to obtain
Rights, in new lands espied.

Thus Jacob and his comrades true,
Turned westward, toward the Oblong's vale.
Eager the trail to find, pursue,
Found homes none assail.

Tilled by the sturdy Pioneer,
The virgin soil surpassed in yield.
And as the record would appear,
Content was bred in field.

The generations came and went,
Ambitions each for greater stores,
Rich blessings, multiplied were sent,
In children, flocks by scores.

Until, with passing of the years,
Since early settlers blazed the way,
Our number, never in arrears,
Proclaims we're here to stay.

Thus, spreading wide, the family tree,
Its outstretched arms enfold
The generations, eight, you see,
These records now have told.

From city, town and distant states,
Are gathered here relations, all,
With name, and age, and sex and date,
And stories some recall.

Go little book, to homes away,
With past and present blended.
Point out the branch since Jacob's day,
From which we are descended.

---

[1] *Year Book of the Dutchess County Historical Society*, October, 1915—October, 1916, p. 45.

[2] John Polhemus and Richard Polhemus, "Up on Preston Mountain", *Poughkeepsie Sunday Courier*, November 12, 1922. See also Harlem Valley Times, December, 1931.

[3] Arthur T. Benson (compiled by), *Jacob Benson, Pioneer and His Descendents: In the Towns of Dover and Amenia, Dutchess County, New York and Elsewhere*, (Poughkeepsie, NY: A.V. Haight Company, 18 & 20 Liberty Street), 1915.

[4] Ibid.

[5] John Polhemus and Richard Polhemus, Ibid. and *Harlem Valley Times*, Ibid.

[6] *Harlem Valley Times*, Ibid.

[7] Arthur T. Benson, Ibid.

Centennial Celebration History Shorts 1914–2014

The following essays are also a part of the Centennial Celebration section of the Yearbook, but, unlike the four preceding essays which took as their topics the history of the Dutchess County Historical Society or related subjects such as the Dutchess County Society in The City of New York, Franklin Delano Roosevelt and his interest in preserving history, or Arthur T. Benson, an early member of the Dutchess County Historical Society; the essays that follow are all focused more broadly on Dutchess County in the hundred-year period from 1914 to 2014.

We put out a call for papers asking for short essays about families or businesses that had been in Dutchess County continuously for the hundred years from 1914 to 2014, the same period that the Dutchess County Historical Society has been in operation. The call was directed especially at city and town historians and historical societies. We have been pleased with the result—and a bit surprised as well. We are happy to present ten short articles on a variety of topics. These constitute mere snapshots of life in the county; there is no attempt to present a comprehensive view of life here during the hundred year period. Yet, some themes do stand out: for example, the waning influence of agriculture over the decades, the growth of business, and the persistence of many families in the area. I would like to thank everyone who participated in this effort. — *The Editor*

The Abels
of the Town of Union Vale

by Dr. Stephen Abel
Submitted by Fran Wallin, Town Historian, Town of Union Vale

Figure 1. *View of Abel Family Home in Union Vale with land of Abel's Trees surrounding. Photograph by Stephen Abel. Collection of Dr. Stephen Abel.*

The Abels were some of the earliest settlers in the Town of Union Vale. Their arrival dates back to the late 1700s, before Union Vale was formed from parts of Beekman and Freedom. William Abel, born in 1751, is buried at the historic Emigh stone house in Clove Valley with his wife, Sarah Emigh. His father and grandfather had emigrated from the Palatine region of Germany.

As time passed, many descendants migrated to other regions of the state and country but others remained in the Clove Valley. In 1850, William W. Abel (1814–1892) purchased the property on North Clove Road where his descendants still live today.

The Abels were primarily farmers in Clove Valley and over the years owned and farmed numerous different properties in the Clove. Over the years different individuals pursued other interests in addition to farming. Several Abels also taught school locally, in addition to engaging in their agricultural endeavors. Orlin Burr Abel (1845–1914) for example, went all the way to Fayette, Iowa, to attend college at Upper Iowa University during the Civil War. A college graduation program shows that he gave the Salutatorian address in Latin in 1865. When he returned home, he continued to farm, in addition to teaching school. In the early 1900s, his son, Claude Abel (1881–1966), was one of the first people in the country to keep and raise Dutch Belted cattle.

Figure 2. *Claude and Mary Abel. Photograph. Collection of Dr. Stephen Abel.*

In 1926, Claude went to the Danbury State Fair where he became very intrigued with the Easy spin-dryer washing machines. He purchased three and brought them home with him, giving one to his wife, and demonstrating and selling the others. When they were gone, he continued to get more and, with time, expanded his product line to include most major household appliances. For over eighty years, many county residents relied on Claude Abel and Son for their household appliances and repairs. The business became Vincent's (1915–1993) primary occupation, but he still continued working the farm. In the 1960s, the Abels had the largest flock of sheep in Dutchess in addition to raising chickens, pigs, horses, and cattle.

Figure 3. *The Abels at a family gathering in the summer of 1941. Photograph. Collection of Dr. Stephen Abel.*

Figure 4. *View of evergreen trees planted at Abel's Trees. Photograph by Stephen Abel. Collection of Dr. Stephen Abel.*

Several generations were actively involved in local government and served in a number of positions including town supervisor, justice of the peace, postmaster, revenue collector, and town clerk.

In the 1960s, Vincent began planting thousands of evergreen trees in many fields that were no longer needed for pasture or hay production. Although the original intent was to plant for reforestation and lumber production, this endeavor evolved instead into a choose-and-cut Christmas tree business that still continues today as Abel's Trees. Vincent also created one of the landmarks of North Clove Road when he dug the 38-acre lake, Lake Vincent, whose scenic beauty is enjoyed by many passers-by today.

The farm is currently operated by me (Stephen Abel) and my adult children. We continue to manage the farm that was first purchased by William Abel in 1850; my grandchildren will be the seventh generation to live on the same property and the eleventh generation in the Clove. I am a veterinarian who practiced in Madison County, Iowa, for thirty years before returning home to live on the farm and currently work here in Dutchess County at Hudson Highlands Veterinary Medical Group in Hopewell Junction.

In 2007, an agreement was made with the Dutchess Land Conservancy to protect the Abel property from any future development and preserve for everyone the natural beauty of the property.

The Andros Family, Residents of Dutchess County since 1893, Working for the Railroad

by Jacqueline Andros Homko

Submitted by Patsy N. Costello, her Cousin
President, Town of Hyde Park Historical Society

According to the Ellis Island database, my grandfather, Giacomo Colaruotolo, left Italy at the age of fourteen and arrived in New York on June 16, 1893. Giacomo might have come to the United States at such an early age because his father had come here before him, but this can't be verified. We only know that, according to the 1900 census, his father lived in Poughkeepsie with Giacomo and his wife, Pasqualina. No further evidence of Giacomo's father could be found and he probably returned to Italy. Ten years after Giacomo had arrived here, his 21-year old brother, Damiano Colaruotolo, joined him. Although Giacomo means James in English and Damiano means Damian, Giacomo's name was changed to John; Damiano's name was changed to Thomas; and their last name was changed to Andros because (as the story goes) their boss couldn't pronounce or spell their Italian names, so he gave them new Americanized versions.

In 1899, Giacomo married Pasqualina Amedio in St. Peter's Church, then located at 95 Mill Street in Poughkeepsie. The next record of Giacomo is the U.S. census of 1900 that shows he was living with his wife and father, next door to the Church, at 109 Mill Street. This address is of particular interest because, when I was growing up in the 1940s, this area around Mill Street was the "little Italy of Poughkeepsie." According to author Christine Scivolette, Poughkeepsie records show that the first presence of Italians was in 1888 when four families settled at 109 Mill Street.[1] Similar information was found on the website for the Italian Church of Our Lady of Mount Carmel, which is now located in what had been St. Peter's Church:

> In 1888, the first wave of Italian immigrants arrived in the Hudson Valley. Seeking to practice the faith they had brought with them from their ancestral homeland, they were allowed to worship in Saint Peter's Church basement. Those first few families had settled nearby in a

house at 109 Mill Street, Poughkeepsie, and they soon welcomed other Italians to the neighborhood.[2]

By 1910, Giacomo had moved from the City of Poughkeepsie (Figure 1). "John Andrews" is listed in the census of that year as a Hyde Park resident living with his wife and five children: Joseph, Elisabeth, Margaret, Anthony, and Rocco (though misspellings occur). This census also lists Giacomo's brother as "Tommie Andrews" living in Hyde Park with wife, Rose. At that time both men worked for the New York Central Railroad. By the 1920 census, three children had been added to John's family: Ann, Fred, and Lillian, and Tom's family had increased to four children: Elizabeth, Frances, Frank, and Felice (Phillip). Another child, Mary, came later.

Figure 1. *The John Andros Family of Hyde Park, N.Y., 1912. Left to right: Margaret, Elisabeth (twins), Pasqualina (mother), Anna, John (father), Joseph, baby Fred, Rocco, and Anthony.*

John and Pasqualina settled to raise their family on River Road in Hyde Park. Originally they lived in a house built in 1850 that they leased from the railroad. Mr. Vanderbilt, their neighbor, had a new house built and the old one torn down. John eventually purchased the new house from the railroad and lived there until his death.

My grandfather, as indicated in the 1900 census, could speak English— which, most likely, gave him an advantage to being promoted as foreman of a track crew. As track foreman for the New York Central Railroad, John was in charge of maintaining a section of the track that was in the vicinity of Hyde Park. For fifteen years he was awarded a prize for having the best section of track in the New York Central System. This is documented in an article about John's 61st birthday celebration that appeared in the February 1, 1940, *Poughkeepsie Eagle News*.[3] In it he recounted some of his 41 years of experiences while working for the railroad, especially the derailing of the famous Twentieth Century Limited, and preparation for the visits of England's King George and Queen Elizabeth to Hyde Park at the invitation of President Roosevelt.

By 1972, it was estimated that members of the family had 238 combined years of railroading.[4] John's four sons followed in his footsteps, beginning as water boys for the track crews, working their way up from the section gang to such jobs as handling baggage, and selling tickets. Rocky worked as a telegrapher for a while and was eventually promoted to freight agent in charge of the Poughkeepsie and West Shore, including Kingston, until he retired. Tony was a track foreman like his father before him, and Joe was a station agent in Castleton-on-Hudson. An article in the *Hyde Park Townsman,* 1988, documents the recollections of Rocky Andros and his railroading experiences as he talked about the "good old days."

John Andros died in 1958 in Rhinebeck, New York, when he was 79 years old. According to his obituary, he had worked for the railroad for 50 years. His wife, Pasqualina, died in 1965 in Hyde Park. John and his brother Thomas, who died in 1974, left a long line of descendants, some of whom still live in Hyde Park and many others within the County of Dutchess. The family property on River Road in Hyde Park is currently owned by Peter J. Andros. It incorporates Hyde Park Landing, the marina near the Hyde Park Railroad Station. (See the website: www.hydeparklanding.com.) Patsy Newman Costello, daughter of Margaret Andros Newman, is president of the Town of Hyde Park Historical Society. Several other cousins also live in the area.

---

[1] Christine Scivolette, "Italians in the Hudson Valley." Accessible at http://www.theitalianclub.com/Newsletters%20Archive/TIAHA_September_2006_newsletter.pdf

[2] "History of Our Lady of Mount Carmel," 2005, n.p., Web. Website, 2005.

[3] "Colaruotolo Has Birthday," *The Poughkeepsie Eagle News,* February 21, 1940. Accessible at http://fultonhistory.com/newspapers%20Disk3/Poughkeepsie%20NY%20Daily%20Eagle/Poughkeepsie%20NY%20Daily%20Eagle%201940.pdf/Poughkeepsie%20NY%20Daily%20Eagle%201940%20-%200155.pdf

[4]   "Andros Family Achieves 238 Years of Railroading," *Poughkeepsie Journal*, August 18, 1972, p. 8, web. May 10, 2014, Newspaper article.

Zimmer Brothers Jewelers and the Poughkeepsie Tower Clock

by Michael D. and Deborah Zimmer Gordon

In 1858, when Poughkeepsie was surrounded by rolling land and the sound of a church bell could be heard for more than a few miles, an important landmark was erected on the southwest corner of Main and Little Washington Streets in the center of downtown Poughkeepsie, NY; the New First Reformed Church (Figure 1) was dedicated on September 7, replacing the old church which had been destroyed by fire the preceding year, on January 18, 1857.

The Tower Clock

The new church was a magnificent edifice with a 65-foot tower that contained a four-faced clock (Figure 1). Its six-foot dial, which could be seen from practically anywhere in the city, and the sound of its huge bell soon became well known. The clock became known as the "tower clock" and later the "town clock." The church became known as "the town clock church." In October 1913, there was another major change: the congregation of the First Reformed Church decided to join the congregation of the Second Reformed Church and moved in with them on Hooker Avenue, Poughkeepsie. After the last service in the tower clock church on October 12, 1913, the clock was given into the care of the Poughkeepsie Common Council.

Figure 1. *The New First Reformed Church at the corner of Main and Little Washington Streets in Poughkeepsie, NY. With four-sided Tower Clock and church bell, built 1858. Photograph. Collection of Michael and Deborah Gordon.*

The common Council maintained the clock and passed a

resolution declaring it the official city clock. The empty church stood until late in 1919 when it was torn down to make way for the construction of the Strand Building. In early 1921, the clock was relocated into the tower of the Strand on the same site at Main and Little Washington Streets.

History of Zimmer Brothers Jewelers

Meanwhile, we shift our attention to the firm of Zimmer Brothers Jewelers. Zimmer Brothers was founded in Poughkeepsie in 1893 by Thomas J. Zimmer, Jr. Thomas began his jewelry career as an apprentice in Poughkeepsie at the age of fourteen. He became an accomplished manufacturing jeweler and moved to New York City. In the city, Thomas became shop foreman for the former George O. Street Co., a firm known widely in the trade for their fine quality and craftsmanship. While at George O. Street, Thomas specialized in work for Tiffany & Co. Thomas returned to Poughkeepsie and, in 1893, opened his first store. A few years later, he was joined in the business by his brother, Fred, a Master watchmaker.

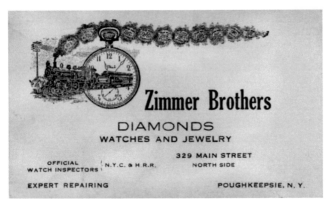

Figure 2. *Business card of Zimmer Brothers store, 1918. Photograph. Collection of Michael and Deborah Gordon.*

After Fred's Untimely death in 1911 at the age of 49, Thomas bought out his late brother's interest in the store and was joined by his youngest son, Leonard Sr. in 1914 (Figure 2). Leonard was a graduate of the Philadelphia School of Horology where he had learned watchmaking, hand engraving, and jewelry manufacturing. Leonard eventually took over the business and guided it through the perils of the Depression years and World War II.

Leonard Sr.'s oldest son, Leonard Jr. joined the firm in February 1948. In those years, Zimmer's windows (Figure 3), along with the artful skill of Leonard Jr. as a jeweler, became recognized in the Mid-Hudson area.

Figure 3. *The Christmas window display, 1963. Photograph. Collection of Michael and Deborah Gordon.*

Zimmer's won a number of national awards and industry-wide acclaim. After Leonard Sr. passed away in 1962, Leonard Jr. continued to run the business. In 1970, Leonard's older daughter, Deborah, married Michael Gordon; he joined the firm a year later.

The Vicissitudes of the Town Clock and Rescue by Zimmer Brothers

In 1924, the city contracted with Zimmer Brothers to take care of the winding and servicing of the huge clock. this arrangement worked very well and three generations of Zimmers made the weekly trek up the tower to wind the weights that drove the heavy gears. When the church was torn down, the large 4,000-pound bell was removed. The bell, cast in Sheffield, England, just prior to its installation in 1858, was not reunited with the clock in the Strand Building.

In the late 1950s, the city lost interest in maintaining the clock. The Colonial Theatre organization erected a large steel and neon sign on the east side of the tower, covering the east face of the clock, thus, cutting two of the Roman numerals off and using the clock's steel frame as a support for their sign.

Early in 1972, as the Strand Building was being demolished, the old clock got a reprieve. Poughkeepsie Jeweler, Leonard Zimmer Jr., grandson of the first Zimmer to wind the clock, climbed up the tower along with his son-in-law (the author), and saved the three undamaged faces of the clock. It was an eleventh-hour rescue, the kind you see in the movies, with the wreckers' shovel bucket taking bites out of the southwest end of the building, that old tower swaying and groaning with each bite. A wet mixture of snow and rain was falling that made the task a bit more difficult.

The most well-preserved of the faces of the clock was painstakingly restored by hand by Mr. Zimmer himself. New hands were cut from cedar wood to the exact measurements of the weather-ravaged originals. A pattern of the clock was made on paper and new panels, cut from a frosty Lucite, were cut and fitted to replace the opaque glass. The new electric movement was custom-made by a Massachusetts firm and fitted into the building. On August 24, 1973, the Poughkeepsie tower clock was installed on the face of the newly enlarged and remodeled Zimmer Brothers Building on the Main Mall (Figure 4).

Figure 4. *Façade of the Zimmer Brothers Jewelers store on Main Street, Poughkeepsie, 1974, with the installation of one face of the Tower Clock. Photograph. Collection of Michael and Deborah Gordon.*

On September 5, 1973, the Poughkeepsie Common Council unanimously resolved "that the restored 'Poughkeepsie Tower Clock' now situated on the face of the Zimmer Building overlooking the Main Mall be, and it hereby is, designated the 'official clock' of the City of Poughkeepsie."

Interest in the clock was strong. When word of its restoration was carried by the Poughkeepsie Journal, Zimmer Brothers was deluged with phone calls and letters of reminiscence from people who remembered the grand old clock, each from a different angle and direction as they had grown up.

In 1973, Zimmer Brothers issued a bronze coin, depicting the Poughkeepsie Tower

Clock, in honor of the clock's 115 years in Poughkeepsie and Zimmer Brothers' 80 years; 10,000 coins in bronze and 50 coins in silver were struck. The bronze coins were given to the public at the grand opening of Zimmer's newly enlarged store on downtown Poughkeepsie's Main Mall.

Figure 5. *The Zimmer Brothers store in Arlington section of Poughkeepsie, built in 1986. With one of the faces of the Tower Clock installed on the facade. Photograph. Collection of Michael and Deborah Gordon.*

In 1986, Zimmer Brothers built a new store on Raymond Avenue in the Arlington section of Poughkeepsie and installed a second restored dial from the clock on the front of the building. The third dial was donated back to the Reformed Church, who gave it back to Zimmer's in 2007. This third dial was installed on an interior wall as part of the store's renovation in 2008 (Figures 5 & 6).

Figure 6. *Interior view of the Arlington Zimmer Brothers store with the third, and last surviving, face of the Tower Clock installed on the wall. Photograph, 2013. Collection of Michael and Deborah Gordon.*

Recent History of Zimmer Brothers Jewelers

In the 1970s and later, the business continued to grow with the partnership of Leonard Zimmer Jr. and his son-in-law, Michael Gordon. They opened a store in the South Hills Mall in 1979 and another in the Galleria in 1991. In 2001, Michael and Deborah's daughter, Jocelyn, joined the firm (Figure 7). Jocelyn's eye for fashion and design, along with her excitement and natural ability to connect with customers has added a fresh dimension to the store. Sadly, Leonard Jr. passed away in 2008 after 60 years with Zimmer Brothers Jewelers, but he did have the good fortune to see his son-in-law and grand-daughter working with him in the business he loved.

Figure 7. *Left to right: Leonard Zimmer Jr., Jocelyn Gordon Klastow, and Michael D. Gordon, owner/managers of Zimmer Brother Jewelers, Poughkeepsie, NY, c. 2003-2008. Photograph. Collection of Michael and Deborah Gordon.*

The Passing Scene: Rose Hill Farm, Red Hook's Oldest Family Business

*by Claudine Klose, President of the Board, Historic Red Hook
and Christopher Klose, Secretary of the Board, Historic Red Hook*

"It's a bittersweet time for us," muses David Fraleigh, taking in the rolling hills, ponds and ancient maple trees lining the narrow lane into Rose Hill Farm, in the Town of Red Hook. "There are days I want to sell and days that I don't." It's understandable.

Figure 1. *Sign for Rose Hill, Red Hook's oldest continuously owned and run family business. Photograph. Collection of David Fraleigh.*

Six generations ago, Peter Fraleigh (1773-??) founded the farm. Rose Hill is Red Hook's oldest continuously owned and run family business (Figure 1). In 2001, the New York State Agricultural Society recognized it as one of the state's ten Bicentennial Family Farms, the only fruit farm so honored.

Under the stewardship of David and his wife Karen, it has become a favored Hudson Valley "pick your own" destination, especially inviting for Karen's delicious homemade pies and jars of jam. Sadly, the seventh generation of Fraleighs is not interested in farming.

Rose Hill Farm is up for sale.

It is only fitting then that we salute the family's perseverance, dedication and savvy business sense over more than two centuries. The first Fraleigh to arrive was Peter's grandfather, an indentured immigrant from Palatine Germany who settled in Rhinebeck and by 1719 had worked his way up to freeholder status, leasing a farm on the Beekman Patent.

Evidently, life in the New World agreed with the Fraleighs, enough so that on May 1, 1798, Peter was able to buy the 92 acres that he and Helena Kuhn (his second wife) would name "Rose Hill" upon their marriage in 1812.

George William (1816–1866) succeeded his father, marrying Regina Waldorf in 1839. The New York State Census for 1865 lists them and five children as resident on the farm that year, producing 50 tons of hay, 20 bushels each of oats and rye, 337 bushels of apples, 500 pounds of butter, 2,200 pounds of pork, and 30 pounds of wool.

John Alfred (1841–1914), their industrious second son and the farm's next steward, took over upon his father's death. In 1871, he married Lucy Irene Curtis (1845–1913) and they began to diversify, starting a long-running door-to-door milk route in the Village of Red Hook, and adding a third story and plumbing to the farmhouse to accommodate summer boarders.

Figure 2. *Elmore (1909–1995) and Ruth (1913–1995) Fraleigh, c. 1916, on Rose Hill Farm's maple-shaded lane. Photograph. Collection of David Fraleigh.*

Stays on scenic farms like Rose Hill, within easy rail distance of New York City, were popular with late-19th Century vacationers. In the *Red Hook Journal* for the 1894 season, the Fraleighs advertised Rose Hill as "pleasantly located at an elevation. Perfectly healthy, plenty of shade, extended views in all directions… hot and cold water throughout the house."

John and Lucy's children, Curtis (1872–1944) and Rosalie (1875–1956), grew up in the bustle of late-century Rose Hill. They delivered the milk before school, tended to the "guests" (as boarders were termed), and looked after the farm's numerous quacking, clucking, mooing, neighing, barking, oinking, and baaing two- and four-footed denizens.

Typical of Fraleigh men, Curtis married later in life—at 35, in 1907. With his father's death on the eve of World War I, he and his wife, Fannie Keys Elmore (1884–1954) ushered the farm into the twentieth century, including welcoming the fifth generation—son Elmore (1909–1995) and daughter Ruth (1913–1995) – into the world (Figure 2).

On the business side, they stopped dairying, ended the milk route, and expanded fruit production, especially apples. They continued hosting city folk, including a "Miss Elizabeth Smith," whom the *Rhinebeck Gazette Advertiser/ Red Hook News* of July 10, 1920, noted "has been spending her vacation at Rose Hill Farm as a guest of Mrs. Curtis Fraleigh."

Figure 3. *The fourth and fifth Fraleigh generations gather in the 1930s on Rose Hill Farm, Left to right, top: Dr. Harvey Losee, Curtis Fraleigh, John Losee, Rosalie Fraleigh, Fannie E. Fraleigh; bottom: Elmore Fraleigh, Ruth Fraleigh, Lawrence Losee. Photograph. Collection of David Fraleigh.*

As the Jazz Age, "talkies" and the Roaring Twenties stormed through America—even Red Hook!—young Elmore ventured off for four years of math and physics and a degree from Wesleyan University. But in 1931 with jobs hard to find in the Depression, he was back on the farm with his father, raising sheep, some poultry, and more apples and other fruit (Figure 3).

Father and son successfully managed Rose Hill through the '30s and World War II. Curtis passed on in 1944 and Elmore took the reins, marrying Barbara Saxon Rutherford (1917–2007) in 1945. The next year he added twenty acres of new orchards, beginning a rise to the top of local fruit production that was to culminate in his being named Grand Champion fruit grower of the 1973 Dutchess County Fair.

To supplement farm income, Elmore served as a Red Hook town justice for some 20 years, worked at the Red Hook Cold Storage and at the post office, and drove a Red Hook Central School bus. He was a member of the Farm Bureau, Red Hook Grange, and the Hendrick Hudson Masonic Lodge.

Before leaving for Cornell and a degree in fruit production, Elmore and Barbara's middle child, David, struck a deal with his father about the future of Rose Hill. "'It's either me or the sheep,' I told my Dad," David recounts, smiling. "I hated them!"

David took over in 1979, first selling apples only wholesale. He and Karen were married in 1984 and that first year together they planted 3,500 dwarf trees – in three days! They switched to "pick-your-own" in 1994, starting with a retail fruit stand. They planted more "reachable" apple trees, added peaches, cherries, strawberries, blueberries, pumpkins—practically anything to satisfy what David says is "people's amazing desire to reconnect with the land."

Despite lamenting that they have very little time now other than to put out fires, David and Karen agree they're right in line with their ancestors: "We offer the complete family experience."

"We want people to come here to see where their fruit comes from and who grows it. That's been our direction."

In 1998, they sold the development rights to the farm under an arrangement worked out with the Scenic Hudson Land Trust. "We're only stewards," says David. "There was nothing better we could do for Red Hook."

And what of the future? "It will take a pretty rare person to appreciate what's here. We'll see how it all shakes out."

McCabe & Mack LLP Law Firm

by Candace J. Lewis

One of the oldest law firms in Dutchess County, McCabe & Mack has been in practice for over one hundred years. John E. Mack opened his law practice in Poughkeepsie in 1896. Throughout his career, he was active as a politician and local civic leader. Born in Arlington in 1874, probably on the Vassar College campus where his parents were employed, he grew up in an Irish-American family. The original family name may have been Mc-Namarra and been shortened to Mack. John Mack graduated from Pough-keepsie High School, then read law in the office of John Hackett, James L. Williams, and Allison Butts, the "Hackett Law Mill." He would establish and sustain a law practice that lasted until his death in 1958. Tall and thin, he often appeared wearing a black suit, a broad-brimmed black hat, and a Lincolnesque string tie.

Figure 1. *Franklin Delano Roosevelt and John Mack behind WKIP radio microphones. Photograph. Collection of McCabe & Mack LLP.*

John E. Mack also enjoyed a distinguished career of public service. He became District Attorney in 1906, a post he would hold for six years. Before Mack's tenure, it was the custom for the D.A. to permit local constables and Justices of the Peace to handle ordinary crimes and the D.A. to concern himself only with the murders and other more serious cases. A great deal of local crime in the county went unnoticed except by the victims. Mack and his staff gave new time and attention to crime fighting—hiring a car to get to the scene of the crime and using physicians in criminal cases. The higher costs were questioned, but the supervisors and citizens were happy with the results.

John Mack and Franklin Delano Roosevelt, both devoted members of the Democratic Party in Dutchess County, were longtime friends. Mack was present and possibly instrumental in Roosevelt's first political speech – at a policeman's clambake in Poughkeepsie in August 1910. Roosevelt later reminisced,

> In front of the courthouse I ran across a group of friends of mine. As I remember, they were Judge Morschauser, George Spratt, John Mack, and Judge Arnold. I had only intended to stay in town for a few minutes to do some errands, but they kidnapped me – one of the first cases of deliberate kidnapping on record – and took me out to the policemen's picnic in Fairview. On that joyous occasion of clams and sauerkraut and real beer—on that great occasion I made my first political speech...

In 1932 and again in 1936, Mack was chosen to place the name of his friend Franklin Delano Roosevelt in nomination for the Presidency of the United States.

The McCabe firm began when Joseph A. McCabe was admitted to practice in 1914. Born in 1890 and a graduate of Poughkeepsie High School, McCabe graduated from Fordham Law School in 1913 and was admitted to the bar in 1914. Although he did not read for the law at the Hackett Law Mill as did John Mack, he started his working career with that office. McCabe served as an enlisted man, a machine, gunner, in World War I and spent time as a prisoner of the Germans. He established his own practice after the war. He was known as a book lawyer, famous for beautiful briefs and thorough research. He was brilliant and careful and was a lawyer's lawyer when a colleague had a difficult question.

In 1974, the two firms merged on the strength of a one page letter agreement between Joseph C. McCabe, the son of Joseph A. McCabe, and John

E. Mack's son Edward J. Mack. The merged firm, McCabe & Mack, initially occupied 42 Catherine Street. As the firm grew with the addition of partners and mergers, it required more space. After deciding to remain in downtown Poughkeepsie, in 1985, the firm, now with over twenty lawyers, built the building it currently occupies at 63 Washington Street.

Today the firm has nine partners and another fourteen lawyers on the roster as associates or of counsel. The non-attorney staff currently numbers twenty-two. A full-service law firm, McCabe & Mack is the largest Dutchess County law firm and one of the area's leading practices. The firm represents clients throughout the Hudson Valley, from New York City to the Albany area, in state and federal courts. Clients include banks, insurance companies, developers, manufacturers, not-for-profit organizations, municipalities, and service companies as well as many small businesses. In 2011, the Dutchess County Historical Society awarded the firm its Business of Historical Distinction Award.

A History of the Battenfeld Family and Battenfeld Farm from 1914 to 2014

by June Gosnell
Town Historian, Town of Milan

The Battenfelds have been family farmers in Dutchess County for more than one hundred years. Conrad Battenfeld and his wife, Elizabeth, came to America from Germany in the 1880s and established their farm on Milan Hill Road in the Town of Milan. The Hudson River with its steamboats and nearby railroad stations provided access to markets in New York City. Battenfeld raised fruit, vegetables, livestock, and a family. Later their cash crop was fruit trees.

Figure 1. *Fred Battenfeld standing in front of glass work area that used sunlight before electricity. 1930s.(The gas pump was installed in 1929.) Photograph. Collection of Fred Battenfeld.*

In the 19th and early 20th centuries, the violet flower was very popular. Raising violets on a commercial basis became a profitable industry in the Hudson Valley. As the industry grew, farmers in Northern Dutchess, including the Town of Milan, decided to raise violets. In 1906, Conrad Battenfeld's sons, Frank and Fred, built greenhouses, raised and shipped violets. By 1912, Milan had fifteen violet growers. For years, the violet was the most popular flower in America. Frank and Fred did very well growing violets. Later Frank left to open a grocery store, leaving Fred to expand the farm that would remain in the family.

After the First World War, the violet industry began to decline and, by 1929, the Battenfelds were one of only three violet growers left in the Town of Milan. In the 1930s, during the Depression, having saved some money, the Battenfelds purchased their present farm, with original greenhouses, located on Route 199 in Milan's Hamlet of Rock City (Figures 1-4).

Following World War II, most of the Hudson Valley violet greenhouses closed down. The Battenfelds continued to grow violets while beginning to raise another flower, anemones. In 1956, third generation Richard Battenfeld, started full production of hybrid anemones which were shipped fresh-cut from the farm in wholesale and retail quantities (Figures 3 & 4).

A few Dutchess County growers were still growing a small amount of violets to carry on the family tradition. One of them was Richard Battenfeld who grew a few hundred violet flowers "for old times' sake."

Fred Battenfeld, fourth generation, with his son and daughter Lance and Morgan, fifth generation (Figures 5-7), now operate the family farm, growing Christmas trees, hybrid anemones, and one narrow bed of a hardy, deep purple violet, Frey's Fragrant.

Figure 2. *Richard Battenfeld and greenhouse workers. 1930s–1940s. Photograph. Collection of Fred Battenfeld.*

Battenfelds is the world's largest growers of hybrid anemones, one of the oldest Choose and Cut Christmas tree farms in Dutchess County, and, as far as they know, the only remaining area still growing the Frey's Fragrant variety of violet on the East Coast.

For over 100 years, the Battenfeld Farm has been a vital part of the beauty and economy of the Town of Milan and Dutchess County.

Figure 3. *Original Battenfeld greenhouses in snow. 1930–1940. Photograph. Collection of Fred Battenfeld.*

Figure 4. *Interior of an old greenhouse, showing flats of violets being tended by workers. 1930–1940. Photograph. Collection of Fred Battenfeld.*

Figure 5. *Aerial view of Battenfeld Farm showing Christmas trees growing around the central buildings of the farm. Photograph. 2014. Collection of Fred Battenfeld.*

Figure 6. *Aerial view of greenhouses and main house at Battenfeld Farm, Town of Milan, Hamlet of Rock City. Photograph. 2014. Collection of Fred Battenfeld.*

Figure 7. *The Battenfeld family in the business in 2014.*
From left: Lance, Morgan, and Fred. Photograph. Collection
of Fred Battenfeld.

The Hermans Family of Northern Dutchess County Farming, Insurance, and Books

by Sarah K. Hermans

My ancestors first arrived in New Amsterdam in 1660 and made their way to what would become Kingston, New York. In the early 1800s, William Hermans of Kingston crossed the river and started a family with Catherine Rowe and lived in what would become the Town of Milan in Northern Dutchess County. Although the family has been in the county for a long time, I would like to tell the story of the Hermans in Northern Dutchess during the last one hundred years—1914 to 2014—a tale of constant challenge and some success.

Figure 1. *Jacob Luther Hermans with grand-daughters Louise and Madge at the farm near Jackson Corners in the Town of Milan, c. 1915. Photograph. Collection of Sarah K. Hermans.*

In 1914, William's grandson Jacob Luther Hermans, Jacob's son Clayton Hermans and his wife Bertha Kilmer, and their two infant daughters Louise and Madge lived and worked a farm on Academy Hill Road near Jackson Corners in the Town of Milan. Jacob purchased the farm in 1876 from Peter Pells who had purchased it from Jeptha Wilbur in 1828. It is said that Wilbur bought the land from one of the original patentees of the "Little Nine Partners." The Hermans farm produced peaches and apples and other fruit, and the family subsisted from cows, pigs, chickens and produce.

A son, Walter Clayton Hermans, was born in 1915 to this small but hard-working family. Even before the stock market crash of 1929 and the ensuing Great Depression, they struggled with farming, an industry that had sustained them and their neighbors for generations before. In 1924, Clayton found work laying flooring in Brooklyn and the family moved to Queens, in New York City, but kept the farm in Dutchess County. Though Walter and his sisters graduated from high school in Queens, they returned to the farm in the early thirties and continued the operation.

In 1932, the daughter of another local farming family, Mrs. Irene Pulver Duxbury (a divorcee, graduate of Vassar College, and Millerton Grange member) began selling National Grange Insurance as a way to support herself. Walter Hermans married Mrs. Duxbury's niece, Helen Pulver, in 1938. In April of 1945, Walter joined the Navy and guarded the bridge over the Croton Reservoir. During this time, he was also a park ranger for the Taconic State Park in Millerton at Rudd Pond (a distant cousin, Charles Hermans is currently in charge), and later he ran a sand and gravel business from the farm on Academy Hill. In the mid '50s Walter had a wife and four children to think about and so he decided to take an opportunity to join his wife's aunt Irene in the insurance business. Duxbury & Hermans Insurance Agency was born. As Mrs. Duxbury was in her seventies at this point, Walter bought the business from her for an agreed down payment and payments of $100 a month for the rest of her life. She lived to be 92.

The agency has always been based in Millerton, New York (where Aunt Irene was born), though it has moved around town several times. For a short while, a branch of the agency was operated from Pine Plains by Walter's wife, Helen Pulver Hermans. Walter's youngest son, John Luther Hermans, newly married to Marty Losee from Rock City (and of the Losee family of doctors and academics from Upper Red Hook), entered the family business in the early '70's and became agency principal when his father retired in 1979. Marty Hermans joined the business as office manager and bookkeeper in 1984 once her children were both in school. Their son Jacob Luther Hermans worked for the agency for a time before relocating to Charleston, South Carolina, and I joined in 2004. Today, as John and Marty prepare to retire, I am taking over my mother's responsibilities and the agency enters its eighty-second year in business. Its office can be found at 66 Main Street in Millerton.

In 1975, Walter Hermans's oldest son Dick Hermans opened Oblong Books in Millerton. Oblong opened a second location in Rhinebeck in 2001, and Dick's daughter Suzanna Hermans (who had been helping at the store since she was a child) joined him in 2007. Today, Suzanna is co-owner of this family business and is the current president of the New England Independent Booksellers Association.[1] Though the retail bookselling industry is going through difficult times, she and her father run a flourishing, locally owned, independent bookstore which hosts talks, book signings, and other events.

As for the family farm, the acreage stayed in the family until just after Walter's death in 1994, but the farming business had petered down to nothing more than a small herd of black-faced sheep. Though agriculture—the industry our family relied upon for generations—was no longer viable by the mid-twentieth century, the Hermans family has established and continues to run prosperous, local family businesses that have allowed us to remain in Dutchess County into the twenty-first century.

Figure 2. *The 50th anniversary of Duxbury & Hermans, Inc., 1982. From left : Walter C. Hermans, Helen P. Hermans, John L. Hermans. Photograph. Collection of Sarah K. Hermans.*

---

[1] For more about Oblong Books, see http://usatoday30.usatoday.com/life/books/news/2011-02-10-1Abookstores10_CV_N.htm

The History of the Grinnell Library

by Mary Schmalz
Town Historian, Village of Wappingers Falls

It all goes back to Irving Grinnell. Born in 1839 into a prosperous New York City family, he retired young to lead the life of a gentleman of leisure on his estate, *Netherwood*, located in what is now Bowdoin Park. Grinnell took a Victorian philanthropist's interest in Wappingers Falls. In his efforts, he was aided and abetted by his friend, the assistant minister and later minister of Zion Church, Henry Yates Satterlee, who came to Wappingers in 1865, left the area in 1881 and went on to become the bishop of the National Cathedral in Washington D.C. in 1896. During his time in Wappingers, Grinnell was instrumental in several "village improvement" projects, one of which was the establishment of a library.

In 1867, the two men established a Circulating Library and Reading Room at the corner of Market and East Main Streets. They charged a dollar a year for membership, and hired a local widow, Elizabeth Howarth, to take care of the books and clean the rooms.

Figure 1. *The Grinnell Library on East Main Street, Wappingers Falls, New York. Completed in 1887. Inspired by Irving Grinnell, a New York City businessman retired to Dutchess County. Designed by Henry M. Congdon (1834-1922), an architect from Newburgh, New York. Photograph by Candace Lewis.*

By 1880 the library was outgrowing its space and was in perpetual need of funds. A building fund was started, but it didn't take off until 1885 when Grinnell held a Lawn Party and a Union Fair was held at Zion Church, both in aid of the library. The lot at the corner of East Main and Spring Streets was purchased in 1886; construction began and was completed in 1887.[1]

Grinnell hired a New York City architect and supplied a list of architectural features he wanted to include. The tower is modeled after one he saw in St. Battenberg, Switzerland, and the way to the second story overhangs the first recalls buildings he liked in Chester, England.

Grinnell Library was chartered as an association library in 1888, making it the sixth oldest in the state.

The library was in what is now the upstairs reading room, with an entrance by way of the winding staircase in the turret. The main room below it was rented, first to a jewelry store and later—after 1926—to a clothing store. The store's door was in the middle, still marked by the stone arch.

At the western end of the building, a second entrance led to a rental apartment upstairs and the offices of the local newspaper, the *Wappingers Chronicle*, downstairs. The *Chronicle* also rented the basement for their printing plant. The building was lighted by gas until 1912, when it was electrified. A photograph taken before a hot-water heating system was installed in 1923 shows a wood-burning stove piped into the eastern chimney.

Grinnell died in 1921 and in his will created an endowment fund for the library. In 1923 the collection was re-catalogued and classified. A representative came from the state Board of Education and analyzed the collection, removing about 2,000 books on the grounds that they were out of date, in bad shape, or contained "no literary merit." One of the apartments, which had fallen vacant, was converted into a children's room and furnished by the Reese family. In 1924 the library became a "Free Library" under state law.

The library was a hundred years old in 1967, and to celebrate, the library took over the remainder of the building and installed carpeting and air conditioning as well as bookshelves and other furniture. At this point the Clapp paintings were collected, restored, and hung throughout the building. The upstairs reading room was named in honor of Margaret Mesier Reese and the room we now use for a storytelling room was refurbished by the Kiwanis Club for use as a meeting room. What is now the director's office was a Music and Arts Room.

In the next decade, the library expanded again when the Aldrich addition was built. This comprised what are now the children's room upstairs, the reference room downstairs, and the community meeting room in the basement, more than doubling the previous floor space. With the coming of computers, it was necessary to rearrange again, stationing the public computers in the reference area and the Children's computers upstairs in the children's room.

In 2009, the Storytime Room was renovated to provide a beautiful and welcoming environment for the many children and their families who attend our weekly story times. In 2011 the Turret was transformed from the original spiral staircase, which is not safe for public usage, to a functional and user friendly reading room.[17]

---

[1] The Grinnell Library, 2642 East Main Street, Wappingers Falls, NY 12590, (845) 297-3428, www.grinnell-library.org

The History of Rhinebeck Bank

by Candace J. Lewis

One of the oldest financial institutions in Dutchess County, Rhinebeck Bank, formerly known as the Rhinebeck Savings Bank, traces its beginnings to the year 1860 when it first opened for business in the town of Rhinebeck, New York. Today, while the bank retains its allegiance to Rhinebeck, it has moved its headquarters to Poughkeepsie, the county seat, with branches all over the county and beyond, thus serving the entire county and Mid-Hudson area. Along with savings and mortgages, the bank offers its customers commercial banking, personal and commercial insurance products, and investment and retirement planning.

On April 12, 1860, Rhinebeck Savings Bank was incorporated as a mutual savings bank, opening its doors for business on Saturday, May 5, 1860 (Figure 1). At first, banking was only conducted on Saturdays from 3:00 to 8:00 pm and checks were not accepted as deposits. Mary S. Gillender was the first depositor that day with $100. The day's total deposits added

Figure 1. *The original Rhinebeck Bank building , 14 Montgomery Street, Rhinebeck.*

up to $511. The first mortgage granted was on July 1, 1870, for $8,000 toward the purchase of a residential dwelling. From that point on, mortgage investments of Rhinebeck Savings would fulfill the dream of homeownership for thousands of local families.

In 1883, Rhinebeck Savings purchased land at 14 Montgomery Street in Rhinebeck for $2,000 as the site for the permanent headquarters. Permission was granted by the State Banking Department on September 14, 1884, and construction of the one-story brick building was completed in 1885. The location remained the headquarters until 2001.

In the early 1970s, the Village of Rhinebeck was struggling economically as retail trade relocated to outlying areas. Rhinebeck Savings made a bold investment and constructed the Rhinebeck Savings Village Plaza in the heart of the community. Opening in November 1974, it consisted of four two-story buildings to house local stores and business offices. The project stands as a lasting legacy of the Bank's leadership and commitment to the future of the local service area.

Over the years, the bank expanded its branches to better serve its customers throughout the Mid-Hudson area. The bank opened branches in all parts of the county and even across the Hudson River: Millerton (1974,

Figure 2. *Rhinebeck Bank headquarters at 2 Jefferson Plaza, Poughkeepsie, NY 12601.*
Inset image: *Michael J. Quinn, President and CEO, Rhinebeck Bank.*

then sold in 1994), Hyde Park (1980), Red Hook (1995), South Road (1999), Arlington and Mid-Hudson Center branches (2000), Rhinebeck Branch Renovation (2003), Kingston (2006), East Fishkill (2007), Beacon (2009), and LaGrange (2010). During this extensive period of expansion, perhaps two of the most significant events were the move of Headquarters to 2 Jefferson Plaza in Poughkeepsie (Figure 2) and the transformation of Rhinebeck Savings Bank into Rhinebeck Bank, a holding company, with retention of 100% of the shares.

In 2012, the Dutchess County Historical Society presented the bank with its Business of Historical Distinction Award for its service to the community.

A major Dutchess County landmark through its people, its service, its commercial activities, and its many branches, the Rhinebeck Bank proudly displays its motto: "We're local. We're involved. We're responsive."

100 Years Ago:
A Transformative Year

by Colton Johnson

Figure 1. *James Monroe Taylor, President of Vassar College (1886–1914). Photograph. Vassar College Libraries/Special Collections. During Mr. Taylor's presidency, the enrollment tripled to nearly 1,000 students.*

Nineteen-fourteen was a transformative year for Vassar College. In February 1913, college President James Monroe Taylor (Figure 1) had announced plans to retire, "definitely not later than February, 1914," according to *The New York Times*. A popular and skilled leader since assuming office in 1886, President Taylor had recently faced criticism from students, faculty and alumnae, despite his critical contributions to the college. In his first years, he had resolved a financial crisis and severe decline in enrollment, caused in large part by the continuance of the college's preparatory division and by the challenges posed by Smith and Wellesley, which had opened in 1875. Taylor had closed the preparatory division; increased and steadied enrollment at 1,000; funded and constructed some dozen buildings including the Library, the Chapel and six residence halls; enlarged library holdings, from about 12,000 volumes to some 80,000; built a strong and growing endowment; and established a dozen faculty chairs in fields ranging from history, economics and political science to biology and psychology—all of them relatively new disciplines.

But these accomplishments were, by 1914, offset in many minds by Taylor's admitted "conservatism," which he traced in 1909 in an essay, "The Conservatism of Vassar," to John Raymond, the college's president when it opened in 1865. Looking back in 1875, Raymond had declared, "the mission of Vassar College was not to reform society but to educate women." Vassar's "single purpose," Taylor argued, was "to maintain and advance the standards for the education of young women" and "not to be led aside…by any of the alluring or insistent demands…which are better suited to the mature than to those in the process of education." To his critics, this conservatism explained Taylor's obduracy to discussion at Vassar of such issues as woman suffrage and to a more democratic organization of the faculty.

When Taylor stepped aside in February 1914, no successor had been found. The trustees' executive committee and the administrative offices assumed control of the business and day-to-day matters, and the faculty asked for—and, in an extraordinary gesture, were given—responsibility for academic matters, including discipline and the development of the curriculum. Along with Professor of History, Lucy Maynard Salmon, and other senior colleagues—some of them alumnae, such as Professor of English, Laura Wiley Johnson '77, Professor of Greek, Abby Leach '85, and Professors of Astronomy, Mary W. Whitney '68 and Caroline Furness '91— the appointed faculty chairman, Professor of Economics Herbert Mills, took immediate advantage of this opportunity, reorganizing the faculty, extending suffrage within that body, establishing a faculty committee for conferring with the trustees and asserting the faculty's right to a voice in educational policy. In the process, the faculty—and, surprisingly, the trustees' executive committee—approved formation of a student Suffrage Club. On July 24, 1914, *The Poughkeepsie Evening Enterprise* said:

> Being without a president six months has given the faculty…an opportunity to get together and to discuss openly as never before the needs and policies of the college. From the start Miss Salmon has been the ringleader.

This changing campus environment awaited the new president, Henry Noble MacCracken, whose election was announced on December 15, 1914, and who took office on February 1, 1915 (Figure 2). The son of the former chancellor of New York University, John Mitchell MacCracken, he held degrees from New York University and Harvard. Having interrupted his university studies for three years of teaching at the Syrian Protestant College in Beirut—later the American University in Beirut—he had also studied at Oxford. A member of the Smith English department at the time of his appointment, he foresaw the challenge awaiting him at Vassar in two departmental colleagues, the brilliant and sternly traditional department chairman, Mary Augusta Jordan, and her progressive and equally formidable associate, Mary Augusta Scott—both members of Vassar's Class of 1876. As he recalled in his book, *The Hickory Limb*, "Since both Miss Scott and Miss Jordan were Mary Augusta, the talk at department meetings consisted chiefly of 'Mary Augusta, you are mistaken.'"

Figure 2. *Henry Noble MacCracken, President of Vassar College (1914--1946). Photograph. Vassar College Libraries/Special Collections. President MacCracken took the helm at Vassar College and remained there during much of the first half of the twentieth century. Unlike his predecessor, he was seen as a leader who was open to the wider world and open to change. He vowed to "make Vassar students citizens of the world."*

MacCracken came to Vassar and to Dutchess County with a broad sense of the world and of contemporary issues, and from the outset his educational mission was, as he put it, to "make Vassar students citizens of the world, beginning with Poughkeepsie." Also he didn't see students as maturing learners requiring protection from dispute or propaganda; students were, in effect, "the college, and the rest of us, trustees, teachers, and staff, were their servants, not parental substitutes."

Speaking to the New York alumnae at the Hotel Biltmore on January 29, 1915—his first public address to a Vassar audience—the president-elect coined a new word to explain another provocative concept, according to *The New York Times*. The term "student activities," he said, suggested that "the process of learning through merely official ways were necessarily 'passivities,' I prefer today to use the phrase 'extra-curriculum'…and to include under it all processes of learning and invigoration of body and mind which are not reached within the somber, black-boarded walls of the classroom."

> One might be tempted to say, [he continued] after a review of college life in many ages and countries, that curricula may come and go, but the extra-curriculum goes on forever…. Nothing that is now a matter of form in the college curriculum was not once the product of the burning resolution of students to possess themselves of that knowledge from which they were withheld.

> We teachers have to learn [he concluded] that the extra-curriculum activities of the student body represent the life-giving source of the college world. It is for us teachers and scholars to realize this…and thus to set the youthful mind free for another forward step in the advance of true culture.

Although his inauguration was deferred to coincide with Vassar's fiftieth anniversary celebration in October, MacCracken lost no time in setting new directions for the college. Speaking to the Philadelphia alumnae in March 1915, he acknowledged the need "for more new buildings," but called for a million dollars, "The Fiftieth Anniversary Fund," for better faculty salaries, additional faculty and an educational endowment for the library and lecture funds. In April, although unable at the last minute to speak, he endorsed a "Peace Meeting" on campus sponsored by the Suffrage Club and the Socialist Club. And in June, according to *The Vassar Miscellany,* he commended the work of the student/faculty committee of the Good Fellowship Club House—a facility opened on campus in 1908 to develop and support the educational and leisure activities of a self-governing organization of campus maids:

> It is democratizing; it is definite; it offers a concrete answer to those who impugn the good will of our altruism; it gives an excellent practice to beginners in teaching and organizing.

In their first year at Vassar, the MacCrackens also entered local life. In 1916, he and his wife Marjorie founded Lincoln Center, a community service center in Poughkeepsie, and also that year he served as the founding president of the Dutchess County Community Health Association, the first such organization in the country, (his vice president was Sara Roosevelt, the mother of the Assistant Secretary of the Navy). The MacCrackens' settling into Vassar and Dutchess County, however, coincided with the

Figure 3. *Vassar students participate in 1914 "Class Day" activities, 1914. Photograph. Vassar College Libraries/Special Collections.*

deepening of the war in Europe, giving McCracken obligations away from the campus. A founding member in 1915 of the League to Enforce Peace, he came to the attention of President Woodrow Wilson, and, at Wilson's request, in 1917, he ended his brief service as head of the Division of Instruction of the New York State Council of Defense to found and head the American Junior Red Cross.

Adjustments to the curriculum demanded by World War I led to the Vassar Training Camp for Nurses in the summer of 1918—418 college graduates from 117 American colleges and universities completed a year's work toward the nursing degree, thus aiding the post-war recovery—and it gave a model for the more complex modifications undertaken during World War II. These included additional, specialized classes, accelerated graduation and, after the war, the accommodation of nearly one hundred male veteran undergraduates. Such accommodation to national life is reflected, nearly one hundred years later, in Vassar's coordinate program with West Point and to the current matriculation at the college, through the Posse Foundation, of military veterans.

MacCracken's international experience led to his bringing students to the college from Central Europe in the 1920s and to his relocation of distinguished scholars to Vassar and elsewhere in the United States during the rise of the Third Reich and the closing of European universities. Thus, international education and academic exchange entered Vassar's ambit in their earliest days.

One of MacCracken's less successful innovations also bore fruit in later years. The euthenics program, undertaken in the 1920s with a group of alumnae and a few professors with the aim—in the words of his biographer, Elizabeth Daniels—of "modernizing women's liberal arts education and training women in a scientific and interdisciplinary way for a life of active citizenship and community participation, "ultimately failed to find an audience. But, a few decades later, Vassar led in adapting the concepts of multidisciplinary studies and experiential learning to the liberal arts curriculum. In the shorter term, MacCracken translated much of the pedagogy and techniques devised for the euthenics program into his planning, with William Lawrence, for Sarah Lawrence College, which opened in 1926, with MacCracken as chair of the board of trustees and Marion Coats as the new college's founding president.

Henry Noble MacCracken retired in 1946. Thus begun, however, his innovations and his connections of the college with the county, the country, and the world continued throughout his presidency and until today. Building with confidence on the firm foundation laid by his predecessor, endorsed in 1914—remarkably—by a conservative board of trustees, consistently buoyed by an ever more progressive alumnae body and always reliant on "the burning resolution of students to possess themselves of…knowledge," he created the modern exemplar for Vassar College.

ADDENDA

Contributors

Stephen Abel can trace his genealogy to more than twelve different families all living in the towns of Union Vale, Beekman, and LaGrange prior to the Revolutionary War. After living in Italy with the American Field Service student exchange program in 1971-1972, he went to college at Iowa State University and received his Doctor of Veterinary Medicine in 1979. He practiced in a large mixed animal practice in Madison County, Iowa, for thirty years prior to returning home in 2007. He currently works part-time at Hudson Highlands Veterinary Medical Group in Hopewell Junction and spends the rest of his time managing the farm and the Christmas tree operation.

Bob Clark received his Bachelor and Master degrees in History from Texas Tech University. He worked as an archivist at Texas Tech's Southwest Collection until 1991. He then attended Syracuse University College of Law, graduating with a Juris Doctor in 1994. Bob practiced law in New Mexico from 1994 to 2001. He returned to the archival profession in June 2001 when he joined the staff of the Franklin D. Roosevelt Presidential Library and Museum as an Archivist. He was the Roosevelt Library's Supervisory Archivist from February 2005 until May 2014, when he was named the Library's Deputy Director.

Harvey K. Flad is Emeritus Professor of Geography at Vassar College in Poughkeepsie, New York. Dr. Flad's scholarship has focused on cultural and historic landscapes, artists of the Hudson River School, environmental and urban planning, and urban history. His work in film, video and photography has included the prize-winning film *Hyde Park*; an on-line essay on landscape photography for the Smithsonian Institution's *Click!* Series; and as writer and narrator of the 2006 DVD *A Digital Tour of Poughkeepsie*, reissued on the Vassar College You Tube site in 2010. He is coauthor with social historian Clyde Griffen of *Main Street to Mainframes: Landscape and Social Change in Poughkeepsie* (Albany: SUNY Press, 2009).

Deborah Zimmer Gordon, daughter of Leonard Zimmer (deceased), wife of Michael Gordon, and mother of Jocelyn Gordon Klastow (three principals in the firm of Zimmer Brothers Jewelers), is an accomplished writer, events planner, and gardener. She is the great granddaughter of Thomas Zimmer, one of the founders of Zimmer Brothers (in 1893). The Zimmer family emigrated to this area from Germany 185 years ago and has been here ever since. Her granddaughters are the seventh generation in Dutchess County. Her mother's family was also in the area for generations and, at one time, owned the property which is now Innisfree. The lake there is named Tyrrell from which that side of her family is descended. Ms. Gordon has volunteered and served on the boards of many local non-profit organizations and was instrumental in founding the Beatrix Farrand Garden Association of which she has been a longtime board member as well. She adds that she was the first licensed female color video camera operator in the U.S.A. in 1969.

Michael Gordon. A U.S. Navy Vietnam veteran, Michael attended Merrimack College and is a graduate of the Connecticut School of Broadcasting. Arriving in Poughkeepsie in 1968, he was a D.J. on WKIP and WHVW in Hyde Park. Michael joined his wife Debby's family business, Zimmer Brothers Jewelers, in 1971 and now serves as president of this 121-year-old firm. Michael is a founding director and serves on the board of Riverside Bank in Poughkeepsie, the Arlington Business Improvement District board, The Pleasant Valley Planning board, and the Board of the Dutchess County Historical Society.

June Gosnell is the former Town Historian and a twenty-seven-year resident of the Town of Milan. She is the daughter of Lt. Thomas F. Darby, a New York State Trooper, who was stationed in Dutchess County for seven of Franklin Delano Roosevelt's presidential years in office. During that time Lt. Darby as a young trooper, was assigned to Troop "K" Details whenever President Roosevelt came home to Hyde Park, some of the most memorable guarding Roosevelt's estate, assignment to the 1939 visit of King George VI and Queen Elizabeth, and to President Roosevelt's funeral in 1945.

Eileen Mylod Hayden is the granddaughter of a founder, John J. Mylod, and daughter of an early member, Frank V. Mylod, of the Dutchess County Historical Society. She herself has devoted most of her career to the society, serving as the first female president of the board (1984-1989) and then as executive director (1991-2007). She is married to Dr. Benjamin Hayden III.

Sarah K. Hermans is the descendant of many Dutchess County families including Fraleigh, Losee, Pulver, Knickerbocker, and Killmer to name a few. Her interest in genealogy came too late to work with her grandmother, Clara Losee (1917-1997), a former Milan Town Historian. She is the current Regent of the Chancellor Livingston Chapter, National Society Daughters of the American Revolution in Rhinebeck. She has a B.S. from Ithaca College and is the office manager at her family business, Duxbury and Hermans Insurance in Millerton. Her uncle is Dick Hermans of Oblong Books fame and her father is John Hermans, CIC, who is also on the board of trustees of Rhinebeck Bank.

Jacqueline Homko was born in Poughkeepsie and graduated from (the old) St. Peter's School on Mill Street. By the time she was ready for high school, her family had moved to Hyde Park and she attended F.D.Roosevelt High, which was then located on Haviland Road. After graduating, from Cornell University in Ithaca, NY with a B.S. degree, Jacquie went to work for General Foods which was in Tarrytown, NY. While there, she met her husband through a co-worker and they began a family of three children while living in Ossining. They moved to Poughkeepsie when husband, Robert, a CPA, was hired by Central Hudson as a tax specialist. They celebrated their fiftieth wedding anniversary last year (2013). Jacquie writes: "So many of the places I was associated with no longer exist as they were so many years ago. It is said that nothing is constant but change, and it is a joy to know that some of the history of the past is being preserved by the DC Historical Society for future generations."

Julia Hotton is the former Assistant Director, responsible for education, at the Brooklyn Museum. She is retired from the New York Public Library Schomburg Center for Research in Black Culture as curator and manager of its Art and Artifacts collection, and there she also directed educational and cultural programs in African American history. As an independent curator, Ms. Hotton has organized a variety of art and historical exhibitions for the New York Historical Society, the Mariners Museum in Newport News Virginia, Syracuse University, and Manhattan East Gallery of Fine Arts. Julia Hotton is a member of the Board of the Dutchess County Historical Society.

Colton Johnson. Professor Emeritus of English and Dean Emeritus of Vassar College, Colton Johnson joined the Vassar faculty in 1965. A specialist in Anglo-Irish literature and an editor of the work of William Butler Yeats, he retired in 2004. In 2013, he succeeded Vassar's founding college historian, Elizabeth A. Daniels (Vassar graduate 1941).

David Johnson. In 1998, at the time of the original publication of "Poppies from Heaven: 1928," David Johnson was an author, photographer, and educator. He wrote to the original publication, *WWI Aero*, that he was working on the geology and hydrology as well as the Lines of Nasca in southern Peru.

Kimberley Jones, the creator of the painting of the Hudson River shown in this issue, is an artist presently living in San Francisco. Ms. Jones is a native of the Hudson Valley. She returns to the area several times a year to visit her parents who live in Poughkeepsie, often using the trip as an opportunity to explore the natural landscape. Ms. Jones is a graduate of the Yale School of Architecture. In recent years, she has shifted her attention from architecture to painting.

Claudine and Christopher Klose are passionate about local history. Claudine Klose is the president of the board of Historic Red Hook and her husband, Christopher , is the secretary of the board. Christopher was a public relations professional in Washington, D.C., for thirty years and now edits a magazine for the National Library of Medicine. Claudine is a retired museum manager who spent the majority of her career at the Smithsonian's National Museum of American History. They now live full-time on the Klose family farm which adjoins the Fraleigh's Rose Hill farm (the subject of their essay in this issue).

Cynthia M. Koch is Public Historian in Residence at Bard College, Annandale-on-Hudson, NY on assignment from the Office of Presidential Libraries, National Archives and Records Administration. She was Director of the Franklin D. Roosevelt Presidential Library and Museum in Hyde Park, New York, 1999-2011. A native of Erie, Pennsylvania, she holds a Ph.D. and M.A. in American Civilization from the University of Pennsylvania. Her most recent publication is "Franklin Roosevelt's Dutchness: At Home in the Hudson Valley" in *Dutch New York: The Roots of Hudson Valley Culture*, ed. Roger Panetta (New York: Hudson River Museum/ Fordham University Press, 2009). She is married and lives in Clinton Corners, New York with her husband, Eliot Werner, president of Eliot Werner Publications, and their two cairn terriers.

Candace J. Lewis is an art historian with a Ph.D. in the field of early Chinese art and a secondary area of specialty in nineteenth-century art in America and Europe. She has taught at Vassar College and Marist College. She is a long-time member of the Dutchess County Historical Society. She became a trustee in 2008, president of the board in 2010, and is now serving as editor of the yearbook. She has lived in Poughkeepsie with her husband, attorney Lou Lewis, since 1969.

Lou Lewis is the senior member of the Poughkeepsie law firm Lewis & Greer P.C., which he founded in 1978. A native of Poughkeepsie, he has practiced law in New York State since 1969 and is a past president of the

Dutchess County Bar Association (1992-93), as well as a former trustee of Marist College (1971-91).

Mary-Kay Lombino serves as The Emily Hargroves Fisher 1957 and Richard B. Fisher Curator and Assistant Director at The Frances Lehman Loeb Art Center, Vassar College where she has overseen the contemporary art and photography collections, exhibitions, and publications since 2006. Prior to joining the staff at Vassar she served as Curator of Exhibitions at the University Art Museum, California State University, Long Beach for six years and Assistant Curator at UCLA Hammer Museum for five years. Her recent exhibitions include *The Polaroid Years: Instant Photography and Experimentation* (2013); *Utopian Mirage: Social Metaphors in Contemporary Photography* (2007); *Off the Shelf: New Forms in Contemporary Artists' Books* (2006); and *Candida Höfer: The Architecture of Absence* (2005).

Marcus J. Molinaro is the current Dutchess County Executive, having assumed office on January 1, 2012. At the age of just eighteen, Molinaro was elected to the Village of Tivoli Board of Trustees, and, in the following year, became the youngest mayor in the United States. He was re-elected mayor five times and elected four times to the Dutchess County Legislature. From 2007 to 2011, he served in the New York State Assembly as the representative of the 103rd District.

Melodye Moore is head of the Collections Committee of the Dutchess County Historical Society and serves as a Trustee on the Board. She is a past recipient of the Helen Wilkinson Reynolds Award from the society. From 1979 to 1986, Moore served as director of DCHS, before taking on the job of managing all site operations at the Staatsburgh State Historic Site (Mills Mansion). Since her retirement, she has returned to DCHS as a trustee in 2011.

Leonard E. Opdycke. the former director of the Poughkeepsie Day School (1965-72), spent most of his career as a teacher, in positions ranging from teaching eighth grade in Shreveport, LA, to heading the English Department at the Harley School in Rochester, NY, to teaching writing at Marist College. Throughout these years, Opdycke also pursued a second career as an aviation historian. For more than fifty years (1961-2007), he directed an international organization, WWI Aeroplanes, and edited its two journals. He also built (and flew!) a full-size reproduction of a WWI airplane. A native of Boston, Opdycke received a B.A. from Harvard and an M.A. in psycholinguistics from the University of Rochester.

Caroline Rogers Reichenberg is a lifetime resident of the Town of Dover, Dutchess County, New York. For many years she owned and operated a company which specialized in general excavating and the manufacturing of precast concrete. She has always had a keen interest in history and preservation. She is a charter member of the Town of Dover Historical Society which was organized in 1974; and served as its president for thirty years. Reichenberg was elected as Dover Town Clerk. During her tenure as town clerk, she is grateful for having had the opportunity to fulfill the very important task of obtaining, and successfully returning to the town, the record book documenting the 1807 organization of the Town of Dover. Now retired after twenty years as town clerk, Reichenberg serves as the Dover Town Historian Co-Chair and enjoys participating in the Town of Dover Historical Society's effort to preserve and share their heritage.

Mary Schmalz is a long-time resident of Wappingers Falls in Dutchess County. She played a pivotal role in founding the Hudson Valley Ramble. An educator, she has made significant contributions to historic sites and historical societies throughout the county for over twenty years. She is serving as the Town Historian for the Village of Wappingers Falls.

William P. Tatum III has held the office of Dutchess County Historian since October 2012. He earned his B.A. in History and Anthropology from the College of William & Mary in Virginia in 2003, his M.A. in History from Brown University in 2004, and is completing his Ph.D. at Brown this year. His main area of research is Colonial North America under English rule. In addition to his scholarship, Tatum has been involved in historic site and museum programs throughout the east coast and England.

Denise Doring VanBuren currently serves as Organizing Secretary General of the National Society of the Daughters of the American Revolution and is the editor of its bimonthly magazine, *American Spirit*. She previously served as New York State Regent of the DAR, as well as Regent of the local Melzingah Chapter of the DAR. Denise co-authored *Historic Beacon* (1998) and *Beacon Revisited* (2003), and served five terms as the president of the Beacon Historical Society. She currently serves on the boards of directors of both the Dutchess County Historical Society and Locust Grove – the Samuel F.B. Morse Historic Site. In her professional capacity, Denise has spent more than twenty years with Central Hudson Gas & Electric Corporation and is currently the utility's Vice President of Public Relations. She holds an undergraduate degree in Journalism and an M.B.A.

Call for Articles: Yearbook 2015

At this writing in August 2014, we are in the centennial year of the Dutchess County Historical Society. It is one hundred years since a group of fifty individuals gathered together to start the task of preserving history. By that, they meant especially gathering and collecting under one roof documents of the past and preserving old buildings. Foremost in the minds of many of them was the task of preserving documents relating to the Civil War, the cataclysmic conflict of fifty years earlier. It was clear that the memories of that important war would soon be extinguished. And, in fact, we now have, at the Dutchess County Historical Society a significant collection of Civil War documents.

In 2015, we will be looking back over 150 years to the end of the greatest conflict in American history and the one that, arguably, has most shaped our nation. For decades before the first shot was fired at Fort Sumter in the harbor at Charleston, South Carolina, the nation was ripping itself apart over how American life was to be shaped then and in its future. The words from the second paragraph of the Declaration of Independence rang with a clarion call: "We hold these truths to be self-evident, that all men are created equal..." But not all citizens heard the same message. The theme of the Forum section for the 2015 yearbook will be topics relating to the Civil War.

In 2015, as for the last several years, the yearbook will have a variety of sections.

(1) The Forum section, which will have as many good articles as we have to present, will focus on the Civil War and issues pertaining to the conflict in Dutchess County. It may include topics from the more abstract—such as discussions of Abolition, political philosophy, and religion—to quite concrete matters such as the number and disposition of individual soldiers in the regiments from Dutchess County.

(2) The Documentation section will focus on shorter articles about a document or artifact.

(3) We also always want to make provision for articles on any worthwhile research regarding Dutchess County history. We do this in the Articles section.

Please submit your article to me in digital form as a Microsoft Word document. Articles for the Forum and Articles sections should be 2,000 to 5,000 words long. Articles for the Documentation section might be shorter—perhaps 1,000 to 2,000 words. Please submit at least one or two images with captions with each essay. Send the images separately as jpegs (300 dpi or larger). Images may be black-and-white or color. Please send them with the draft, the figure captions indicated in the text (images are not an afterthought). For endnotes, please use *Chicago Manual of Style*.

If you have an idea for an article that you are considering, but are doubtful about, just write to me at clewis1880@aol.com and I will be happy to discuss it. I am hoping for first drafts of articles in hand by April 30. Please note that this is an earlier deadline than last year. I look forward with delight to reading your essays.

— Candace Lewis

Cover Photograph

On the cover of this yearbook is a detail of a panoramic photograph in the Collection of the Dutchess County Historical Society. The entire photograph along with a diagram indicating the identities of some of the people in it are reproduced on the next two pages.

> An outing to the Resident of Isaac S. Wheaton, Lithgow, NY, by the Dutchess County Historical Society, September 15, 1926. Photograph (panoramic). Collection of the Dutchess County Historical Society.

The photograph was taken only twelve years after the first meeting—the founding meeting—of the society on April 28, 1914. By this time, the society had expanded its membership from fifty to several hundred. The pilgrimage was already a popular event as can be seen here. Ladies and gentlemen all piled into their automobiles once a year for an outing to a pre-selected site, usually a mansion with beautiful grounds, for an afternoon tea and meeting. These were gay occasions. The absence of smiling faces in the photograph is not due to the somber attitudes of the participants, but rather to the length of time necessary for the photographer to organize the shot and complete the exposure. It was just too long to hold a smile.

Many notable people are in the photograph. John J. Mylod, grandfather of Eileen Mylod Hayden, former Executive Director of DCHS, was President of the society. His son, Frank Mylod, Eileen's father, is in the picture. He served the society as well. Helen Wilkinson Reynolds, editor of the yearbook for many years and author of 63 articles as well as several books, is shown at the left. Claude Abel, ancestor of Dr. Stephen Abel, one of our authors, is represented. At the right side, dressed all in white or a light-colored garment is Denise Lawlor. She lived here in Poughkeepsie. Her mother is shown behind her. In her estate, she left a provision for moneys to be given to the Dutchess County Historical Society every year. We are still receiving a generous donation from her fund—and very grateful for it. — *The Editor*

John J. Mylod

Frank V. Mylod

Helen W. Reynolds

James Stringham

Dr. J.W. Poucher

Dr. Thomas Mylod Brooklyn

James Lynch

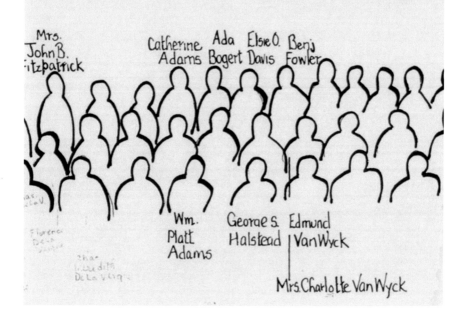

Residence Isaac I. Wheatons - Lithgow, N.Y. S...

Catherine
Sague Miller

Mrs
J.W. Poucher

Ethlyn
Hinkley

Susie
Wiltse

Mrs. George
Waterman

Claude
Abel

George
Uhl

Wilson
Winchester Carpenter

ept 15-1926

Maragret
Brown

Mrs.
Lawlor Miss Denise
Lawlor

Joseph George S.
r VanWyck Halstead

Dr.Alvah Dr James
Peckham Baldwin

John M. Ham

Dutchess County Historical Society

P.O. Box 88
Clinton House, 549 Main Street
Poughkeepsie, NY 12602
845-471-1630
Email: dchistorical@verizon.net
www.dutchesscountyhistoricalsociety.org

John W. & Gloria Golden, Michael & Clare Graham,
Bernard & Shirley Handel, Eileen & Ben Hayden, Steve & Linda Lant,
Maryann Lohrey, Marc Molinaro, Dennis & Marilyn Murray,
Charlie North, Wayne & Bridget Nussbickel, John & Nancy O'Shea,
Eileen & Denny Quinn, Hon. Albert & Julia Rosenblatt,
Mr. & Mrs. Barry Rothfeld, Linda & Steve Saland,
Samuel & Gail Simon, Jim & Joan Smith, William P. Tatum III,
Peter Van Kleeck, Mary Kay Vrba

Staff

Patty Moore, *Acting Director*
Gregory Wiedeman, *Archivist, Project Manager*
Carla Lesh, Ph.D., *Collections Project Manager*
Larry Miller, *Bookkeeper*
Adam Raskin, *Assistant*

Assisting the Staff

Melinda Benanti, Mary Lou Davison, Carol Doran,
Jean Menuez, Tim Smith, Carol Verdis

Review of the Year 2014

Chamber Breakfast, Centennial Celebration. As part of our Centennial Celebration year, we co-hosted , with the Dutchess County Regional Chamber of Commerce, a Breakfast on Wednesday, June 11. Our Trustee, Denise Van Buren, acted as master of ceremonies. The focus was on businesses that had been in continuous operation in Dutchess County for the same period as our Society, i.e. 1914 to 2014. We recognized these businesses and also gave a shout out to multi-generational businesses. A very successful event with 180 in attendance.

Awards Dinner, Centennial Celebration. Plans are in progress for the Annual Awards Dinner, this year reconfigured as a 100-year birthday party for the Society, a Centennial Celebration. The dinner will be held on Thursday, October 23, at the Henry A. Wallace Center, at the Franklin D. Roosevelt Library and Museum, 4079 Albany Post Road, Hyde Park, NY 12538. Trustee, Ann Pinna, is the chair of the event. We expect a great party.

Annual Meeting, Centennial Celebration. In honor of the Centennial Celebration, the Annual Meeting was held April 24, 2014, at the First Presbyterian Church, Main Street, Pleasant Valley, on the same property where the original meeting was held one hundred years earlier, April 24, 1914. Patricia Prunty was elected President of the Board; Lou Lewis was elected to the board and to the position of Secretary of the Board. J. Winthrop Aldrich entertained all assembled with his talk about times gone by.

Yearbook, Centennial Celebration. We are publishing our annual Yearbook, maintaining a tradition established in 1914 with the founding of the Dutchess County Historical Society. This year the featured theme is Thinking Historically, a celebration of our centennial year.

Glebe House. Moneys left over from a government grant to the City of Poughkeepsie ($20,000) were allocated by the Common Council to the Glebe House for repair and painting in the interior of the building. The work was completed this spring. This project was supervised by Julius Gude, Trustee, Head of Facilities, and Gordon Cruikshank, Trustee. This is a huge improvement at the Glebe House following on the heels of the new roof, recently installed at the same location.

Our Centennial Fundraising Campaign continues. Dennis Dengel, brother of long-time Board-member and supporter David Dengel, has pledged $25,000 towards the campaign.

Development. We received a grant from the Lillian Cumming Streetscape Fund at the Rhode Island Foundation for $15,000. We have just received grants from the Community Foundations of the Hudson Valley: the Denise M. Lawlor Fund for $9,000 and the Community Response Fund for $1,000 for a new computer. This year again, as part of the Big Read sponsored by the Poughkeepsie Public Library District, the Society sponsored an essay contest for Middle and High School students.

Collections. Work in Collections has expanded considerably this year with more donations and continuing accessioning and cataloguing of our incoming and existing items. In addition, we applied for and received a grant for $8,000 from the Document Heritage Program of NY State. We have to match the grant. The grant will be for archiving the Hubbard family papers, a collection from an apple orchard family in the Town of Poughkeepsie (business papers, diaries, letters, etc, from 1839 through the 1960s).

Two Lecture Series. In the spring, we ran a lecture series which was very popular. We are co-sponsoring a summer and fall lecture series with the County Historian, Will Tatum: July10 (Underground Railroad), September 18 (Palatine Migration to Dutchess County), and November 6 (Italian immigration in Millbrook).

Big Read Contest. As part of the Big Read sponsored by the Poughkeepsie Public Library District, the Society sponsored an essay contest for Middle and High School students.

DCHS Donors
May 2013 through May 2014

Millennial Circle
Central Hudson Gas & Electric Corp.

Community Response Fund,
Community Foundations of the Hudson Valley

The Denise Lawler Fund,
Community Foundations of the Hudson Valley

Julius and Carla Gude

The Lillian Cumming Streetscape Fund, Rhode Island Foundation

Lou and Candace Lewis

Betsy Kopstein-Stuts and George Stuts

Sponsor
Jonathan B. and Olivia Altschuler

Roger and Alisan Donway

The Handel Foundation

Ronald Huber

Lewis & Greer, P.C.

McCabe & Mack LLP

Marist College

Passikoff & Scott

Dr. Samuel and Gail Simon

Patron
John Ackerman Quinn Financial Services, LLC

Doris Adams

J. Winthrop Aldrich

Battenfeld Farms

John Conklin

Margaret Duff

Michael and Deborah Gordon

Brian Keeler

Marshall & Sterling, Inc.
Poughkeepsie Journal
Poughkeepsie Public Library District
Rhinebeck Bank
Riverside Bank
Albert M. and Julia C. Rosenblatt
Jim and Joan Smith
Roger Smith
Phillip and Barbara Van Itallie
Vassar College

Sustaining

Roy Budnik / Mid Hudson Heritage Center

Verna Carr

Catharine Street Center

Tom Cervone / CR Properties Group, LLC

The Community Foundation of Dutchess County

Denise M. Lawlor Fund

Frederick Doneit

Roland DuSault

Jack Effron

Steve Effron / Efco Products

Michael Elkin

Edwin Fitchett

Gene Fleishman and Judith Elkin

Gloria Gibbs

Handel & Carlini, LLP

Shirley Handel

Health Quest

Hudson Valley Federal Credit Union

E. Peter Krulewitch

Virginia LaFalce

Linda Lant

Edwin Leonard

Mary Ann Lohrey

Cora Mallory-Davis

Tom McGlinchey

James Merrell

Larry Mille

Henrietta Mountz

John Pinna

Poughkeepsie Rural Cemetery

Patricia Prunty

Eileen and Denny Quinn

Caroline Reichenberg, Town of Dover Historian

Andrea Reynolds

Rocking Horse Ranch

J. David Schmidt

Mark C. Tallardy

TEG Federal Credit Union

Vassar College Library

Ron Von Allmen

Richard Wager

Eleanor Weidenhammer

Mary Westermann

Member/contributor

American Antiquarian Society

Susan Adams

Pam Allers

Timothy Allred

Jill Auerbach

Virginia Augerson

Joan Carter

Mark Castellani

Ellen Chase

Ann Constantinople

Mary Ellen Cowles

Andrew Dahl

Mary Lou Davis

John DiDomizio

Robert Dreyer

Gary Dycus

Andrew Effron

Walter Effron / The Three Arts

Vicki Fells

Nancy Ferris

Nancy Fogel

Peter Forman

Charles Foster

Dieter Friedrichsen

Deborah Gamber

Michael Gartland

Arthur Gellert

Annatje Gilbert

Vicky Goldman

Ruth Green

Barry Gurland

John M. Hancock

Timothy Holls

Elaine Hyden

Marny Janson

Jeh Johnson

Molly Jones

Kristin Judd

Stephanie Kelly

Cynthia Koch

Carol Kohan

Barbara Lemberger

Ronald Lewis

Edgar Licis

Barbara Lindsey

James Elliott Lindsley

Roderick Link

Kay Mackey

Debra Meisoll

Suzanne Meldrum

Julie Mirsberger

F. Kennon Moody

Sandra Moore

Arnold & Debbie Most

J.A. Museolino

Gerrianne Nickerson

Louis Northrop

Lauren O'Connor

Richard O'Shea

Jason Oyler

Ann Perry

Viggo Rambusch

Paula Reckess

Fred Schaeffer

Winifred Schulman

David Schwartz

Janice Selage

Celia Serotsky

Ann Shershin

Calvin Smith

Mary & Murray Solomon

Anne Strain

Scott Swartz

Denise VanBuren/Christopher Barclay

Barbara Velletri

Doris Wheeler

Michael Williams

Judy Wolf

Louis Zuccarello

Joseph Ellman

Vicki Fells

Nancy Ferris

Marcia Fishman

Nan Fogel

The Hon. Peter Forman

Charles Foster

Richard Foy

Stephen Friedland

Dieter Friedrichsen

Deborah Gamber

Annatje Gilbert

Gray Crawford Goodman

Jerry Greenberg

Allan Greller

Barry Gurland

John Haas

Haviland-Heidgerd Historical Collection

Janice Hesselink

Timothy Holls

Timothy Holmes

Arlene Iuliano

Monique Jones

Louise Katz

Stephanie Kelly

Matthew Kenny

Linda Kent

Sherrell Andrews Kuhbach and Robert Kuhbach

Lawrence Laliberte

Linda Lant

Edwin Lawless

Barbara Lemberger

Edwin Leonard

Edgar Licis

The Rev. James Elliott Lindsley

Roderick Link

Lucas J. Lucas

Kay Mackey

Andrew Madison

Barbara Markell

Melanie Marks

Carmen McGill

Tom McGlinchey

Shane Medick

Suzanne Meldrum

Carol Menken

James Merrell

Julie Mirsberger

Arnold and Debbie Most

Mount Gulian

Kathy Moyer

Marcia Murray

Drew A. Nicholson

Mary Jo Nickerson

E. Richard O'Shea

Janice Parker

J. M. Perotti

Ann Perry

Viggo Rambusch

Paula Reckess

Fred Roe

Wendy Rosenkilde

Barbara Ruger

Fred Schaeffer

J. David Schmidt

Winifred Schulman

David Schwartz

Janice Selage

Beth Selig

Celia Serotsky

Calvin Smith

Mary and Murray Solomon

Marguerite Spratt

Kathy Sumner

Jon Tallman

Phyllis Teasdale

Town of Hyde Park
Historical Society

Barbara Velletri

Lee Ann Vrablik

Holly Wahlberg

Mary Westermann

Laurie Winfrey

Judy Wolf

Dr. Louis Zuccarello

The Society encourages the use of memorial donations to remember a loved one, or the gift of a special donation in honor of one's birthday, anniversary, or special occasion. Please be assured that all such remembrances will be appropriately acknowledged with a special letter from the Society expressing our sincerest thanks.

It has been the policy of the Dutchess County Historical Society to print only the categories seen above due to space limitations. We certainly value all of our member and donors, including Lifetime, Individual, Family, and Organization. We appreciate each and every one of you. Thank you for your continued support as we move forward into our second one hundred years.

City & Town Historians and Historical Societies of Dutchess County

DUTCHESS COUNTY HISTORIAN

William P. Tatum III
22 Market Street, Poughkeepsie, New York 12601
(845) 486-2381   fax (845) 486-2138
wtatum@dutchessny.gov

DUTCHESS COUNTY HISTORICAL SOCIETY

Post Office Box 88, Poughkeepsie, New York 12602
dchistorical@verizon.net
Patty Moore
(845) 471-1630

CITY HISTORIANS / HISTORICAL SOCIETIES

Beacon
Post Office Box 89
Beacon, New York 12508
Historical Society: Robert Murphy
info@beaconhistoricalsociety.org
(845) 831-0514

Poughkeepsie
62 Civic Center Plaza,
Poughkeepsie, New York 12601
Historian: George Lukacs
saltglazed@aol.com
(845) 471-5066

TOWN & VILLAGE HISTORIANS / HISTORICAL SOCIETIES

Amenia Post Office Box 22, Amenia, New York 12501-5343
  Historian: Arlene Iuliano arlenei@optonline.net (845) 373-9088
  Historical Society: Norman Moore mmoore1776@aol.com
  (845) 373-9338

Beekman 4 Main Street, Poughquag, New York 125700
  Historian: Honora Knox hknox@townofbeekman.com
  Tel: (845) 724-5300

Clinton 820 Fiddlers Bridge Road, Rhinebeck, New York 12572
  Historian: Craig Marshall craigmarshall266@aol.com
  (845) 242-5879
  Historical Society: Mary Jo Nickerson nickersonmaryjo@gmail.com
  (845) 266-3066
  Post Office Box 122, Clinton Corners, New York 12514

Dover 126 East Duncan Hill Road, Dover Plains, New York 12522
Historian: Valerie Larobardier
historianlarobardier@townofdoverny.us
(845) 849-6025
Historian: Caroline Reichenberg
historianreichenberg@townofdoverny.us

East Fishkill Post Office Box 245, Hopewell Junction, New York 12533
Historian: David Koehler healthyharvestcsa@gmail.com
(845) 226-8877
Historical Society: Malcolm Mills bluhilfm@frontiernet.net
(845) 227-5374

Fishkill (Town) Post Office Box 133, Fishkill, New York 12524
Historian: Willa Skinner wskinner30@juno.com (845) 896-9888

Fishkill (Village) 40 Broad Street, Fishkill, New York 12524
Historian: Karen Hitt crotchet@gmail.com (845) 896-8022

Fishkill Post Office Box 133, Fishkill, New York 12524
Historical Society: Steve Lynch asklynch@yahoo.com
(914) 525-7667

Hyde Park Post Office Box 182, Hyde Park, New York 12538
Historian: Carol Kohan hptownhistorian@aol.com
4383 Albany Post Road, Hyde Park, NY 12538
Historical Society: Patsy Costello patsyc97@aol.com
(845) 229-2559

LaGrange Post Office Box 112, LaGrangeville, New York 12540
Historian: Georgia Trott-Herring herringtrott@aol.com
(845) 452-2911
Historical Society: Bob D'Amato
lagrangehistoricalsociety@gmail.com (845) 489-5183

Milan 20 Wilcox Circle, Milan, New York 12571
Historian: June Gosnell jdgosnell@frontiernet.net (845) 876-8363
Historian: Patrick Higgins higginspj@optimum.net (845) 834-2599

Millbrook (Village) Washington (Town)
3248 Sharon Turnpike, Millbrook, New York 12545
Historian: David Greenwood ngreenwd@aol.com (845) 677-5767
Historical Society: Laurie Duncan hsinfo@optonline.net
(845) 677-0323
Post Office Box 135, Millbrook, New York 12545

Millerton / Northeast Post Office Box 727, Millerton, New York 12546
  Historian: Mike Williams willywmike@optonline.net
  (518) 398-6531
  7604 Route 82, Pine Plains, New York 12567
  Historical Society: Ed Downey eddowney@millertonlawyer.com
  (518) 789-4442

Pawling Post Office Box 99, Pawling, New York 12564
  Historical Society of Quaker Hill and Pawling
  Historian (Town): Robert Reilly rpreilly@verizon.net
  (845) 855-5040
  160 Charles Colman Blvd, Pawling, New York 12564
  Historian (Village): Drew Nicholson dan.ddn@comcast.net
  (845) 855-3387
  18 Valley Drive, Pawling, New York 12564
  Historical Society: John Brockway johnbetsyb@comcast.net
  (845) 855-5395

Pine Plains Post Office Box 243, Pine Plains, New York 12567
  Historian: Ann Simmons
  Historical Society: Ann Simmons cas@fairpoint.net
  (518) 398-5344

Pleasant Valley 1201 Netherwood Road, Salt Point, NY 12578
  Historian: Fred Schaeffer fredinhv@aol.com (845) 454-1190
  1544 Main Street (Route 44), Pleasant Valley, New York 12569
  Historical Society: Marilyn Bradford Momof5NY@Yahoo.Com
  (845) 518-0998

Poughkeepsie (Town)
  1 Overrocker Road, Poughkeepsie, New York 12603
  Town Office (845) 485-3646
  Historian: John Pinna ajpinna@aol.com

Red Hook Post Office Box 397, Red Hook, New York 12571-0397
  Historical Red Hook
  Historian: J. Winthrop Aldrich wint42@gmail.com (845) 758-5895
  Historical Society: Claudine Klose claudineklose@gmail.com
  (845) 758-1920

Rhinebeck (Town) Post Office Box 291, Rhinebeck, New York 12572
  Historian: Nancy Kelly kinship@hvc.rr.com (845) 876-4592

Rhinebeck (Village) Post Office Box 291, Rhinebeck, New York 12572
Historian: Michael Frazier michaelfrazier@earthlink.net
(845) 876-7462
Historical Society: David Miller dhmny@aol.com
(845) 750-4486

Stanford Post Office Box 552, Bangall, New York 12506
Historian: Dorothy Burdick No E-Mail Town Office (845) 868-1366
Historical Society: Kathy Spiers lakeendinn@aol.com
(845) 868-7320

Tivoli Post Office Box 311, Tivoli, New York 12583
Historian: Bernie Tieger villagebooks@frontiernet.net
(845) 757-5481

Unionvale 249 Duncan Road, Lagrangeville, New York 12540
Town Office (845) 724-5600
Historian: Fran Wallin franw821@hotmail.com
Historical Society: Henry Kading (845) 677-8174
303 Verbank Road, Millbrook, New York 12545

Wappinger, Town and Wappingers Falls, Village
20 Middlebush Rd. Wappinger Falls, NY 12590
Town and Village Historian: Brenda Von Berg
Town Office (845) 297-4158
Co-Town Historian: Joe Cavaccini Town Office: (845) 298-1150
Co-Village Historian: Mary Schmalz Town Office (845) 430-9520
Historical Society:
Sandra Vacchio info@wappingershistorialsociety.org
(845) 430-9520
Post Office Box 174, Wappinger Falls, New York 12590

Washington Post Office Box 135, Millbrook, New York 12545
Historian: David Greenwood ngreenwd@aol.com
(845) 677-5767
3248 Sharon Turnpike, Millbrook, New York 12545
Historical Society: Laurie Duncan duncan006@optonline.net
Tel: (845) 677-0323

Dutchess County Historical Society
P.O. Box 88
Poughkeepsie, NY 12602
845-471-1630
Email: dchistorical@verizon.net
www.dutchesscountyhistoricalsociety.org

JOIN AS A MEMBER

Throughout the year, the Dutchess County Historical Society sponsors historical trips, lectures, seminars, and workshops about a broad array of topics.

Help support the work of the Society.

MISSION STATEMENT AND GOALS

The Society is a not-for-profit educational organization that collects, preserves, and interprets the history of Dutchess County, New York, from the period of the arrival of the first Native Americans until the present day.

Furthermore, The Society aims:

- To collect, catalogue, and preserve artifacts that make visual and tangible connections to the history of Dutchess County.

- To create permanent and temporary exhibitions, programs, and publications to stimulate interest in the history of Dutchess County.

Glebe House

- To develop program partnerships with other historical, educational, and governmental groups to promote community involvement with the history of Dutchess County.

- To administer Clinton House and Glebe House so as to meet The Society's educational and interpretive goals as well as to preserve the structures and landscape thereof.

- To serve the needs of researchers, educators, students, DCHS members, and members of the general public who wish to study and use the collection.

John Beardsley, first occupant of the Glebe House in 1767 (played by Steve Wing, 2010).

LEVELS OF MEMBERSHIP

Millennial Circle...........$1,000
All benefits listed below plus two tickets to the Gala Awards Dinner

Sponsor...................... $500
All benefits listed below plus two tickets to Living With History Series

Patron......................... $250
All benefits listed below plus a ticket to Living With History Series

Sustaining.................. $100
All benefits listed below plus listing in annual awards dinner program

Family/Contributor...... $75
Includes free library access, annual year book, and invitations to programs and events

Individual.....................$50
Includes free library access, annual year book, and invitations to programs and events

JOIN DCHS TODAY!

Millennial Circle.......$1,000
Sponsor.....................$500
Patron....................$250
Sustaining..............$100
Family/Contributor.....$75
Individual...............$50

Dutchess County Historical Society

Total $ _____

Please send your matching grant forms with your donation.
Many companies match gifts, including IBM.

Name _____

Address _____

City   State   Zip

Phone   email